Rob White
SERIES EDITOR

Edward Buscombe, Colin MacCabe and David Meeker
SERIES CONSULTANTS

Launched in 1992, BFI Film Classics is a series of books that introduces, interprets and honours 360 landmark works of world cinema. The series includes a wide range of approaches and critical styles, reflecting the diverse ways we appreciate, analyse and enjoy great films.

Magnificently concentrated examples of flowing freeform critical poetry.
Uncut

A formidable body of work collectively generating some fascinating insights into the evolution of cinema.
Times Higher Education Supplement

The choice of authors is as judicious, eclectic and original as the choice of titles.
Positif

Estimable.
Boston Globe

We congratulate the BFI for responding to the need to restore an informed level of critical writing for the general cinephile.
Canadian Journal of Film Studies

Well written, impeccably researched and beautifully presented ... as a publishing venture, it is difficult to fault.
Film Ireland

FORTHCOMING IN 2002

The Blue Angel
S. S. Prawer

The Manchurian Candidate
Greil Marcus

Mother India
Gayatri Chatterjee

To Be or Not to Be
Peter Barnes

Vertigo
Charles Barr

I Know Where I'm Going!
Pam Cook

BFI FILM CLASSICS

IVAN THE TERRIBLE
Иван Грозный
....

Yuri Tsivian

 Publishing

First published in 2002 by the
BRITISH FILM INSTITUTE
21 Stephen Street, London W1T 1LN

The British Film Institute
promotes greater understanding
and appreciation of, and
access to, film and moving image
culture in the UK.

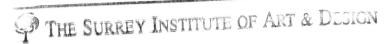
British Library Cataloguing-in-Publication Data
A catalogue record for this book is available from the British Library

ISBN 0–85170–834–X

Series design by
Andrew Barron & Collis Clements Associates

Typeset in Fournier and Franklin Gothic by
D R Bungay Associates, Burghfield, Berks

Printed in Great Britain by The Cromwell Press, Trowbridge, Wiltshire

CONTENTS

. . . .

ACKNOWLEDGMENTS

I thank Naum Kleiman – the acknowledged expert on Eisenstein and *Ivan* – for agreeing to share with me some of his vast knowledge and insight. I am also indebted to Richard Wortman for historical details regarding the coronation of Russian Tsars; to Tom Gunning for his knowledge of Balzac and alchemy; to Joan Neuberger and Ian Christie for their conversations on the subject of *Ivan*; to Evgenii Berstein and Susan Larsen both of whom helped to get straight a difficult section; and to Ed Buscombe and Rob White for their patience. Bradin Cormack, Chris Gilman, Sid Gottlieb, Reinhold Heller, Mikhail Iampolsky, Maureen Lasko, Richard Neer, Simone Tai, and, as always, Roman Timenchik have helped me with their advice at different times – to all of them my thanks; and, of course, to Richard Taylor for reading, and Rob White for editing this book.

For my grandmother Anna Grishina (1900–90)
who did not hesitate to take me to this film.

'IVAN THE TERRIBLE'

. . . .

Introduction: The Film and its Double

Ivan the Terrible is a complex movie – some people even think the most complex movie ever made – not in the sense that its plot is tangled or complicated, but because to embrace it we need to see beyond what the characters say and do. To begin with, *Ivan* is visually complex; then, it has Prokofiev's complex music; and the way Eisenstein structures its story is closer to patterning than it is to narrative progression. It is this triple complexity that this book seeks to address – not to exhaust it, but rather to encourage the viewer to take over next time he or she decides to see the film.

To set the scene, I will start with Eisenstein's political situation, but this book is not really about *Ivan* and history or *Ivan* and politics. Not that this is unimportant, but the quality of the work done in this area by Naum Kleiman[1] and Leonid Kozlov[2] means there is little my book can add to it. In addition, as I am writing this, another little book called *Ivan the Terrible* is being written by the excellent historian of Russia Joan Neuberger: the focus of that book is exactly on Eisenstein's vision (indeed, version) of history. I do not want to make this sound like a tie-in offer, but put together, Neuberger's book and mine cover twice the ground.

Nor am I doing a close analysis of the type found in another excellent book (*Ivan* is fortunate in having so many) written two decades ago by another colleague of mine, the film scholar Kristin Thompson.[3] In the best Formalist tradition, Thompson's enquiry is close to scientific. She begins by isolating her object: *Ivan* as an ensemble of artistic devices, and goes on from there to explain how these are intended to affect the viewer. I have opted for a different angle. My book, too, looks at *Ivan* through the prism of Eisenstein's intentions, but whereas Thompson extracts those from the film's final form, my object is more dispersed: I work chiefly from pre-production documents (notes, sketches, drawings). In other words, what interests me is not so much the film *per se*, but the film in the making, its evolution from scrawl to screen, as it were.

This interest, however, is not descriptive or biographical – I am not writing a biography of Eisenstein's film – my plan is to analyse it in formation. Such an approach as I have attempted in this book can reveal some aspects of *Ivan* which are normally hard to perceive, but it also has its peculiarities. At one point I found myself in a quandary which I believe I managed to turn to an advantage. Not all artists' intentions are equally viable; in the final film, many of Eisenstein's initial ideas are either not found, or found transformed beyond recognition. I wound up with two films on my hands instead of one: one that exists plus its immaterial twin – the film that Eisenstein *wanted* to make. The question is: is this second, phantom movie relevant to our understanding of the first?

If it is, it is for three reasons. First, Eisenstein was not allowed to shoot Part Three, so keeping in view, for instance, how he intended *Ivan* to end is a legitimate attempt at a hypothetical reconstruction. Secondly, Eisenstein's work has always been experimental, and, as it sometimes happens with experimental art, to appreciate the result we need to have at least a vague idea of what could have been the tasks the artist set himself in this or that scene. Finally, I do not think that what we experience when watching a film is impervious to what we know about it. If it is true that our experiences – emotional or visual – depend on our mental set-up, the latter depends on our knowledge. We may admire the child who called the Emperor naked, but a candid eye is of no use to art: the more we know the better we can see. I was eight when I first saw *Ivan the Terrible* (a shattering experience, of which more later), and I am convinced that my present knowledge of how this or that element was intended to work has only sharpened my eye and made that long-established connection with the film more immediate and intense. This gives me hope that this book can serve not only as a historical explanation of Eisenstein's picture but also as a stimulant, an enhancement of viewing experience.

Which does not mean the viewer must read it first. On the contrary, this book reads best after the first viewing. This century made it easier than ever: in 2000 a well-compressed DVD version of *Ivan the Terrible* (complete with outtakes, screen tests and sundry scholarly supplements) became available from the Criterion Collection[4] (beware of other DVD versions!) – the next best thing to a good 35mm film print. With the story of *Ivan* fresh in the reader's mind it will be easier for me to get my point across.

On the other hand, brief priming should help those who wish or are impelled to begin with the book. The following summary is for readers taking the latter option; readers who have a good grasp of the film's story and are familiar with the landmarks of Eisenstein's career may wish to skip it and go straight to the section discussing Ivan, Stalin and Eisenstein.

Plot Summary

Sergei Eisenstein began writing the script for *Ivan the Terrible* in January 1941. This project (which occupied Eisenstein to the end of his life in 1948) was Eisenstein's sixth feature-length movie. Before *Ivan* he made four silent films – one of them famous, three controversial; and a period drama called *Alexander Nevsky*, the popular and official success of which led to *Ivan*, another biographical picture from Russia's past. Between *Nevsky* and *Ivan*, Eisenstein spent time directing a Moscow production of *Die Walkuere*.

Part One. Moscow, January 1547. Inside the Dormition Cathedral Ivan's coronation is in progress. The new Tsar of Russia is seventeen years old. Ivan's two friends, Kolychev and Kurbsky, are shown pouring gold on his head. In his coronation speech Ivan promises to unite the country and root out its enemies. Among those present we see Ivan's aunt Yefrosinya and her son Vladimir; they listen to Ivan with enmity and fear.

In a dark corridor of the Tsar's palace a foreign ambassador incites Kurbsky against his friend: Why is Ivan of Moscow master of Russia, and not Prince Kurbsky of Jaroslav?

In the vast banqueting hall of the Kremlin the Tsar's wedding feast is taking place. The name of his bride is Anastasia. The feast is interrupted: a crowd of rioters (instigated by Yefrosinya and an anti-Tsar coalition of boyars) breaks into the palace. Their leader Maliuta – the Tsar's close associate in the future – brings an ill omen: 'Moscow is horribly bewitched! The bells are crashing down from the steeples!' Ivan's pat answer puts the riot down: 'Witchcraft, you say? Bells falling without reason? A head which believes in witchcraft is itself like a bell – empty! And can a head fall off … all by itself? In order to fall, it has to be cut …'

This scene is, in turn, interrupted by a Tartar envoy from Kazan sent to defy the Tsar. Followed by the crowd of rioters-turned-patriots, Ivan sets out to besiege Kazan. The Russians win the battle.

Upon his return to Moscow, Ivan falls ill – or pretends to, in order to tempt those who aspire to take the throne to show themselves. In a dark corridor of the Tsar's palace Yefrosinya attempts to persuade Kurbsky to take her son's side: 'He is worse than a child. He is moronic. With Vladimir on the throne it is you who will rule as a regent.' Yet Kurbsky, who sees through Ivan's game, swears allegiance to Dimitri, the son of Ivan and Anastasia. Reassured of the loyalty of his friend, Ivan appoints Kurbsky to lead Russian troops against Poland.

Ivan's aggressive foreign policy requires more money to be requisitioned from the Church, and the boyar opposition consolidates around Archbishop Pimen. To weaken Ivan, Yefrosinya decides to poison Anastasia; as she fulfils her plan, the news reaches Ivan that Kurbsky and his troops have been beaten in the Baltics.

Dark interior of the Dormition Cathedral. Widowed and friendless (Ivan's other friend Kolychev had obtained his permission to become a monk in a remote cloister), the Tsar mourns at Anastasia's bier. More bad news is announced as he does so: Kurbsky has fled to King Sigismund of Poland; the boyars are rousing the people against the Tsar. Ivan takes a decision. He will assemble around him 'a brotherhood of iron', as he calls it – people whom he can trust and who are prepared to take an oath against his enemies. Three of them – Maliuta and the two Basmanovs, father and son – stand by as the Tsar keeps his vigil in the dark cathedral.

Ivan's first step is to announce that he is abdicating the throne; this creates a vacuum of power; presently, a long procession of people carrying icons and gonfalons is seen approaching the small monastery where Ivan is now living. At the request of his people, Ivan, crowned the lawful Tsar of Russia at the beginning of Part One, is re-crowned as people's Tsar at the end.

Part Two opens with a scene set in the reception hall at the Polish court. The defector Kurbsky (now Sigismund's vassal) informs the King of Ivan's abdication and of the plight of Russia's troops. Enter a messenger shouting: 'Tsar Ivan is on his way back to Moscow!'

Moscow, the Reception Chamber at Ivan's court. Ivan announces new laws to a group of dismal kneeling boyars: the main power and key border towns will now belong to the crown; internal affairs in the country from now on will be supervised by the Oprichniks – the brotherhood of iron accountable to the Tsar alone.

Anticipating cruelties and purges under the new regime, Philip Kolychev – Ivan's old friend summoned back from the monastery – voices the Church's discontent with Ivan's reforms. There follows a flashback sequence showing a series of scenes from Ivan's childhood which the Tsar recalls to win Philip over to his side: his last glimpse of his mother poisoned by boyars; boyars' misrule in Ivan's name. The flashback ends with the boy-Tsar ordering his huntsmen to arrest the head boyar. Ivan to Philip: 'Stay with me. Help me to re-establish Russian power, and for this accept the office of Metropolitan Bishop of Moscow.' Philip agrees, but on the condition that Ivan gives him the right to plead in favour of the wrongly accused.

The next scene shows the Tsar on his throne, Maliuta perched at the side of it. Swayed by the Oprichnik, Ivan is torn between hatred towards boyars which tells him to act, and the word he has just given to Philip not to punish the innocent. Maliuta offers a way out: 'I'll take the Tsar's sins on my shoulders.' Maliuta will pick victims for pre-emptive purges and execute them. His first choice is a host of boyars from Philip's clan.

Alone, we see Ivan ask himself: 'By what right do you set yourself as a judge, Tsar Ivan? By what right do you wield the sword of justice?' But the next moment he hears a distant cry and rushes to a small secret window giving onto a courtyard where Maliuta is seen in the act of beheading two unbending boyars. When this is over, the Tsar steps out, crosses himself and says: 'Too few! …'

This makes Philip – the former friend – Ivan's extreme opponent. Archbishop Pimen and Yefrosinya urge him to act. One day in the same Kremlin cathedral in which Ivan had been crowned and where we saw him at vigil at the casket of Anastasia, an act of public disobedience is being displayed. As Ivan enters the cathedral in the middle of a mystery play about the biblical tyrant Nebuchadnezzar (a transparent allegory), Philip refuses to recognise him and denies him his blessing. This is the moment when Ivan pronounces the phrase which will become part of his name: 'From now on I will be just what you say I am! I will be Terrible.' This, thus, is Ivan's third, self-proclaimed coronation.

Something in the way Yefrosinya reacts tells Ivan she is guilty of poisoning his wife – as young, handsome and evil Fedor Basmanov had been suggesting to him all along. Meanwhile she and Pimen take a decision to kill the Tsar; a young fanatic, monk Pyotr, is chosen as the regicide. This would make her weak-minded son Vladimir the Tsar of Russia – something the poor youngster does not want and fears. The scene concludes with a lullaby song Yefrosinya is singing to calm him, his head resting in her lap; enter Maliuta to invite Vladimir to the royal banquet.

The banqueting hall, all red, blue and gold (this scene is shot in color). Ivan gets Vladimir drunk so that he blabs about the regicide plot. 'And whom do they want to make a Tsar instead of me?' asks Ivan. 'You will never guess – me,' says poor Vladimir. Another – mock – coronation immediately follows: Ivan orders his regal garments brought in and tells Vladimir to don them. As the mock Tsar (candle in hand) leads Ivan and the procession of Oprichniks from the banqueting hall through the cathedral (the same space where the film began) Petr takes Vladimir for Ivan and stabs him in the back. Another misrecognition follows: as she sees the body spread-eagled on the floor Yefrosinya comes forward shouting: 'Good people, look! Ivan is no more!' As she discovers the truth she goes insane, singing a lullaby while nursing her dead son's head in her lap.

Setting the Scene: Ivan, Stalin, Eisenstein

Since this book is not about history or politics, a few words will suffice to indicate the where and when of the matter. *Ivan the Terrible* is a film shot in the Soviet Union in the first half of the 1940s – the high noon of the Stalinist regime – and under the pressure of Stalin's personal supervision. It was Stalin's idea to commission a film about Ivan IV, sixteenth-century Tsar of Russia (nicknamed the Terrible for carnages and purges), charging Sergei Eisenstein, honoured film director whose political credibility may have had its ups and downs but who was presently (for the time being) in Stalin's good grace, with this task. Worse, among Russia's leaders of the past, Ivan was Stalin's favourite, and this film was to be part of a larger campaign aimed at changing the historical image of Ivan's rule (from 'repressive' to 'progressive') – with an eye to Stalin's own epoch. This may look like it must have been a daunting charge to take on but provided Eisenstein took things easy it was also a 'no-lose' situation. Stalin's taste was known and predictable, and his desire to pose in period settings transparent enough to make Ivan's portrayal acceptable for the sitter even without making it plainly flattering.

The way things turned out was anything but straightforward. Part One gained Eisenstein the Stalin Prize; Part Two was condemned and shelved; consequently, Part Three was never finished (not even rushes have survived, only a screen test and a still or two). The September 1946 official resolution from the Central Committee found two faults with the film: various 'misrepresentations of history', on the one hand, the obtrusive visual style, on the other. What it did not say but makes quite clear was the main thing that went wrong: the parallel between epochs, quite promising at the outset, becomes equivocal as the plot evolves. Politically, Part Two is to this day a conundrum; there is no way Eisenstein did not intend it the way it is, and no way he could hope to get away with what he did.

The resolution further condemned *Ivan*, Part Two, for representing Ivan 'as a spineless and weak-willed character, a Hamlet, of sorts.'[5] In October, Eisenstein tried to save the film (and his precarious political reputation) by publicly acknowledging 'the mistakes of *Ivan the Terrible*'; then, he wrote a letter to Stalin asking for an opportunity to revise and finish the film. The plea was well received. In February 1947, together with the actor Nikolai Cherkasov (the Ivan of the film),

Eisenstein appeared in the Kremlin where their meeting with Stalin, Molotov and Zhdanov was scheduled for 11 at night.

The Kremlin meeting, which took more than two hours, has come down to us as a transcript taken down by Cherkasov immediately afterwards. According to this document, Stalin started off with the famous remark 'Your Tsar has turned out indecisive, like Hamlet',[6] adding a little later: 'Ivan the Terrible was very cruel. You can depict him as a cruel man, but you have to show why he *had* to be cruel.'[7]

> CHERKASOV. Can we leave the scene of [Vladimir] Staritsky's murder in the film?
> STALIN. Yes. Murders did happen.
> CHERKASOV. There is one scene in the script where Maliuta Skuratov strangles Metropolitan Philip. Should we leave that in?
> STALIN. It must be left in. It was historically accurate.[8]

Here Viacheslav Molotov (the Minister for Foreign Affairs) interfered to recap the point Stalin had made earlier on.

> Molotov said that the repressions could and should be shown, but it should be made clear what caused them and why. This required a portrayal of how the state worked rather than scenes confined to cellars and enclosed spaces. The wisdom of statesmanship needed to be depicted.[9]

This was, thus, the political brief, too clear to be of further interest to us: show (was the message) the expediency of repression.

But there was also a minor matter, a grudge against form, which Stalin left to Andrei Zhdanov, then Secretary of the Central Committee, the man mandated to supervise literature and the arts, to express:

> Comrade Zhdanov said that Eisenstein's fascination with shadows distracted the viewer from the action, as did his fascination with Ivan's beard: Ivan lifted his head too often so that his beard could be seen. Eisenstein promised that Ivan's beard would be shorter in future.[10]

This sounds more interesting to look into. We will not find, to be honest, much of a gap between Zhdanov's (Stalin's) criticism of *Ivan* and the way *we* feel towards its self-conscious visuals which many find if not galling then puzzling; does not the action seem indeed to drown in details? There is a lot to say in defence of Eisenstein's preoccupation with shadows and Ivan's manner of cocking his beard, both of which I will address later. Meanwhile, let me give voice to the culprit who was much less willing to cut and trim than his (tongue-in-cheek?) answer to Zhdanov may suggest.

Here is an angry entry that Eisenstein made in his diary on 20 October 1946 (incidentally, on the same day as his all-compliant self-criticism appeared in *Culture and Life*) in which he addresses exactly the type of criticism I am talking about:

> *Overburdenedness* [English in the original] with shadows? The film is crowded with too many images? [But they are 'too many' only] for *those* who do not '*read*' films, but simply hurry on after its action. That is, for those who come to cinema looking for telegraphic syntax, and not for poetic writing with repetitions, visual analogies [*illiustratsii*] and music – for [those who come to the movies for the sake of] the anecdote alone.[11]

This book is not, as I said, about the political history of film – but before we turn to livelier matters, let me summarise two reasons why *Ivan the Terrible* caused official discontent. As a political figure – Ivan's opposite number – the last thing Stalin needed Eisenstein's hero to do was to call into question his right to judge and punish. But Stalin was also an ordinary spectator (not much different from the rest of us) who expected *Ivan the Terrible* to be an enjoyable movie in the ordinary sense. That was the other thing Eisenstein failed, or, as the diary shows, refused to deliver: he refused to see film-making as just another way of telling stories; for him, film was part of the history of art. This was rather quixotic on Eisenstein's part, to refuse to play by the rules of the real world, instead looking for better rules in books, but this is exactly what makes *Ivan* interesting and a challenge to explore. What these rules are, and where Eisenstein found them is what this book is mainly about.

The Credits

One such rule – the rule of a good beginning – Eisenstein owed to Arnold Schoenberg whose article 'The Relationship to the Text' (1912) he quotes in a diary entry made in the summer of 1940. The reason why he would decide, of all things, to reread Schoenberg's old essay discussing the relationship between the music and the lyrics was that, before he took up *Ivan*, Eisenstein was engaged in his staging of Wagner at the Bolshoi, so such issues occupied his mind. The composer of songs, Schoenberg claims, must not 'cling' to the text provided by the poet; on the contrary:

> [I]ntoxicated by the sound of the first words of the text, I had finished many a lied of my own without in the least caring for the further development of the poem, without even noticing it in the ecstasy of composing. Only some days later did I think of looking up the poetical content of my lied. To my great amazement I realized that I could not have done more justice to the poet. The direct contact with the sounds of the first words made me sense what necessarily had to follow.[12]

Having copied this out, Eisenstein goes on to conclude: 'Indeed, the beginning of a text (of a good text) must contain the *nux* [Latin for 'nut'] of emotional imagery which defines the subsequent flow not only of the poem itself, but also of the music written for it.'[13]

The effect Schoenberg's rule had on the making of *Ivan* (which Eisenstein set about six months later) was a special attention paid to the opening credits – a section that would otherwise hardly merit a pause. Visually, the credits sequence is made up of a background of dark wreathing smoke on which first the main title, then the rest of the writings, appears (fig. 1); as for the soundtrack, we first hear an orchestral theme which after a while gives way to a song performed by a male choir. Let me address these four components one by one.

Fig. 1. Credits: the main title printed on the rolling smoke.

The image of smoke which later in the film appears two more times is what a card player might call the 'joker' – a card whose suit and value vary from one deal to another. During the Kazan battle (Part One) the smoke is an index of fires. In Part Two, where this image is used to bracket a flashback to Ivan's childhood, it is more up to the viewer what to think of the smoke (the 'mist' of memory? the subconscious mind?) or whether to think of it at all. In the credits what the smoke stands for is defined by the other three cards in the game: the musical theme, the song lyrics and the name 'Ivan Grozny' written over it.

Western equivalents fail to live up to Ivan's vernacular sobriquet. While words like 'Terrible' or '*Schreckliche*' mean both fearsome and ugly (an association conveyed in Russian by a different word), the word '*grozny*' associates fear with admiration, a mixture inherited from '*groza*' – 'thunderstorm' – from which it stems. This is more than an etymological aside. Like many thinkers of his time, Eisenstein had a faith in 'emotional imagery' buried under the surface of words, and held it to be the task of the artist to restore this imagery to its primal power. To Eisenstein's eyes, the atmospheric image encased in Ivan's name was a case in point: he found it revived in folk songs featuring 'Ivan the Thunderous'; in the biographical legend according to which a terrible thunderstorm broke out on the eve of Ivan's birth;[14] and one preparatory note quotes Alexander Pushkin's line celebrating a later Tsar, Peter the Great: 'The whole of him is like God's thunderstorm,' only to annex the metaphor in favour of Ivan.[15] Thunderstorm was exactly the *nux* – the germ, the nuclear image of the film – which Eisenstein wanted his credit sequence to nutshell.

One way to evoke a thunderstorm was via the sound of thunder – not the natural sound, of course, but indirectly, by means of music. Here, Eisenstein's recent opera experience proved useful. Outlining the musical theme of Ivan – a verbal outline which Sergei Prokofiev was to translate into music proper – Eisenstein instructed the composer to give it a Wagnerian ring: '[M]usically, the theme of Ivan must take the form of an *encroaching* thunderstorm, as though one were to compose a piece entitled "Thunderstorm" (like the beginning of *[Die] Walkuere* – storm, thunder, rain)' and adds: 'This theme must underlie the introductory credits.'[16] Upon contact with Ivan's name (Eisenstein hoped) this music should work to bare the root of the word, releasing its energy.

The fourth element – the song that replaces the music halfway through the credits – has a similar history and a similar charge. In April 1942, Eisenstein jotted two lines of it, a 'dummy' to pilot Vladimir

Lugovskoy, the poet hired to write the lyrics. Imitating the parallelism of folk ballads, the dummy text links the name to its root:

> *Grozy* (Thunderstorms) were encroaching,
> *Grozny* (The Terrible) Tsar rose against them.[17]

Such was the brief; and the following quatrain (rhymed and rhythmed) is what we actually hear from the screen:

> A black cloud is rising,
> The face of the dawn is washed with red blood.
> The boyars' treacherous plot
> Is rising for a battle against the authority of the Tsar.[18]

The original pun is gone – veiled. Instead, we learn about a thundercloud (the first word the viewer hears from the screen) – a verbal image which, in its turn, lends its name (writes up a role, assigns a reading) to a visual one: the black smoke rolling in the background. Thus, interchanging and interacting, the four elements that constitute the credits are made to take part in the making of the fifth – a less material element Eisenstein called a 'motif'.

Motif Structure
Eisenstein wanted to work on *Ivan* in the way Wagner worked with opera and Joyce with prose (to drop two names from Eisenstein's pantheon): giving form and tension to its surface by means of a vast system of internal correspondences, audiovisual 'rhymes', which is what Eisenstein meant by 'motifs'. A motif is, for him, a thing that recurs – an object (figs 2 and 7), a

Fig. 2. The unclaimed coins at the end of the battle will indicate Ivan's losses.

Fig. 3. In Ivan's stateroom: note the chessboard motif.

pattern (figs 3 and 8) – always in a different form and often in a different medium. The golden rain motif, for instance, that links the coronation scene shown in figure 7 with a later one (fig. 2) showing Ivan's soldiers submit a coin each (a form of casualty count), returns in a number of other scenes as a purely musical theme; at least, such was Eisenstein's brief for Prokofiev.[19] To describe it by contraries: Eisenstein's motifs are neither solely ornamental, nor really semantic – not even when they look like allegories, as is the case with the chessboard metaphor (fig. 8) possibly inspired by Middleton and Lewis Carroll.

Nor is any motif in *Ivan* affixed to specific themes, characters or groups of characters; on the contrary, Eisenstein made it a rule to deal them out fairly between *dramatis personae*. This rule ('the rule of ambivalence', we may call it) holds good even for the thunderstorm motif: nominally, it is linked with Ivan, but is not owned by him. For example, if we compare Eisenstein's brief for the credits music with the one he wrote for the song (the two notes I have just quoted) we might observe that the former associates the thunderstorm with Ivan while the latter links it to his enemies. The motif is not an attribute: unlike the conventional 'lightning' that helps the beholder to identify Zeus the Thunderer in mythological paintings, Eisenstein's thunderstorm does not belong to Ivan as a character, but is a property of *Ivan* as a film.

Narrative Structure

Another peculiar thing about *Ivan the Terrible* is that its story develops in a manner similar to the development of motifs. Watching the way in which dramatic situations in *Ivan* parallel, echo, and paraphrase each other, one begins to suspect that most are versions of deeper structures to which Eisenstein ascribed more than merely narrative significance. This suspicion grows into certainty the moment one consults his working records to find most of them listed and named – twin cult, patricide, filicide, bisexuality, birth trauma, the ritual killing of the king. These *ur*-structures – as well as the very idea that beneath the pall of what film characters say or do lurks a deeper truth that concerns us all – stemmed from Eisenstein's interest in monistic theories that held sway in turn-of-the-century psychology and anthropology. These theories all proceeded from an assumption that at the bottom of things there is always a cause – a kernel myth or a primal something: a scene, a trauma.

According to Eisenstein, one key to the story of *Ivan* is the ritual killing of the old king – a rite which the ancients believed ensured the continuity of power. Like many of his contemporaries writing on the subject, Eisenstein held that vestiges of ritual regicide were found in some harmless (and some not-so-harmless) medieval customs, specifically in ones having to do with carnival reversals of power. In a diary entry made in January 1945 he taps such a reversal in order to explain the final scene from the yet unreleased (and yet unbanned) Part Two (the italicised phrase, in English, is Eisenstein's play on the words 'antic' and 'antique'):

> One finds yet another *antic custom* in *Grozny*: *dressing a jester in Tsar's garments and then stabbing him* (in lieu of the Tsar). This, in fact, is the pivot [*bolvanka*] of the entire scene in which Vl[adimir] Andreyevich is killed ('he killed a jester' and 'the fool likes it on the throne').[20]

And pivotal it is. More than once during the sequence, Eisenstein replays the primal situation of regicide, shifting characters and their assumed roles in a carousel of fortunes. The events unfold as follows. Sensing a conspiracy, Ivan invites his young cousin Vladimir to a feast. Drunk, Vladimir confirms that an assassin, Pyotr, has been found to kill the Tsar whereupon he, Vladimir, would ascend the throne – more or less against his own will since he feels he is not made to rule. The scene is set. We have three figures: the king, the pretender, and the killer (now standing in the wings). This first ('real') regicide is averted by its mock reversal. Ivan makes Vladimir don regal garments, puts him on the throne and bows before him in fake reverence. This is the first of two moments marked in the diary entry – 'the fool likes it on the throne' – the moment when a new figure is added to the essential triad: the pretender who poses as the king becomes the king's fool. The other moment the diary refers to accompanies the next reversal of fortune. As Vladimir – still posing as the Tsar but not enjoying the role any more (he feels the game may take a bad turn) – walks, candle in hand, across the cathedral, the killer enters and stabs him in the back. Captured by two guards, Pyotr discovers his mistake and says he is prepared to die. Ivan slowly approaches; holding his arms from both sides, the guards bend the killer into a bowing position; Ivan gestures to him to straighten up and pronounces the line from which the diary quotes: 'Why are you holding him? He did not kill the Tsar, he killed a jester.' What follows looks like an uncanny encore of a previous scene with Vladimir: we watch the king taking a deep bow in front of the bankrupt killer destined to become his friend in Part Three (not destined to be made).

This explains why I find Eisenstein's method of story construction akin to his own way of working with motifs. Here, as there, things only count as long as they recur, but they must recur transformed (the rule of variety) and change hands (the rule of ambivalence). Writing on another subject Eisenstein dubbed such narratives 'telescopic' – at various points, the story returns to one kernel situation, which each time is replayed in a different mode.[21] I have tried to demonstrate the telescopic quality of one sequence, the final sequence of Part Two. If we now change the optical distance and look at Eisenstein's movie as a whole, we see that on the larger scale of the entire film the anatomy of *Ivan* remains essentially the same. Sequences echo, mirror and ape one another; situations turn into their own opposites, lining up telescopic series that span the space of the film from beginning to end.

Fig. 4. Mock coronation at the end of Part Two.

Coronation

One such series involves the sequence discussed above. The mock coronation of Vladimir that concludes Part Two (fig. 4) turns upside down a true one that opened Part One – an unhurried reconstruction of the ceremony marking young Ivan's accession to the throne.

'Reconstruction' is Eisenstein's word, not mine. He used it in a diary entry made in January 1948 (a month or so before his death), comparing, with his usual flair for unexpected juxtapositions, his first film, *Strike*, to *Ivan*, which he knew would be his last – two movies which, on the face of it, could not differ more. The thing in common, he explains, is that both contain quasi-documentary sequences focusing, to quote the diary, on the question '"*how is it done*"' (this in English).[22] *Strike* is what Eisenstein calls a 'tech-film' – a film exploring the technique of underground class struggle. By the same token, the coronation sequence in *Ivan* examines '*how* the anointment is produced' (this phrase sounds as awkward in Russian as it does in translation: Eisenstein wants to present the ceremony as a sort of value-making industry). In both cases, he adds, 'the method is one of reconstruction: [I reconstruct] typical behaviour in typical circumstances.'[23] What interested him most during the staging of the coronation sequence was not so much the theatre of power but, as it were, the factory of power: 'Ritual is the process of production the output of which are non-material, non-object values.'[24] (Those of my readers whose attention I share with Pierre Bourdieu may, at this point, remember his concept of 'symbolic capital',[25] and will not be entirely wrong – though, of course, in this case the capital is feudal.)

Hence the care with which Eisenstein reconstructs two principal rituals of the coronation – robing and gilding – though he does not hesitate to tamper with historical details to makes them better fit the film's design. When we see Ivan receive the orb and the sceptre from the archbishop, for instance, this is done as required by the robing protocol, but when it comes to the ultimate gesture that produces a Tsar, the placing of the crown, he does it with his own hands. This is a departure from the accepted practice, but I think I know the reason why: Eisenstein's Ivan is a self-made Tsar prepared to rule in the teeth of the Church.[26]

The gilding ceremony has also been changed. Eisenstein would have known how this ritual looked from one ancient miniature reproduced in Alexander Nechvolodov's *Tales of the Russian Land*, an illustrated history book which Eisenstein frequently uses as a source.[27] In this picture (fig. 5), we see the newly crowned Tsar's passage from the cathedral (in which the robing ceremony has just taken place) to his

Fig. 5 (left). Sixteenth-century miniature: gold coins are thrown at the new Tsar on the steps to the palace. Fig. 6 (right). Gilding: a sketch.

Fig. 7. Gilding as shown in the film.

palace; his brother Yuri is seen showering golden coins to gild his path. Though one of the sketches for the film (fig. 6) looks fairly faithful to this source, in the actual film we find Ivan standing, not walking, in the centre (and not on the steps) of the cathedral while the shower of coins keeps pouring endlessly upon his head (fig. 7). Small as it may seem, this adjustment alters the original symbolism of the event: the current of coins no longer evokes the path of gold, but a golden rain – one of the motifs of Eisenstein's film.

Kurbsky at the Polish Court

In the opening sequence of Part Two – roughly halfway between the straight coronation and its mock reversal – we are shown another theatre of power, only this time Eisenstein parodies rather than reconstructs its workings. The props are a sword and a knightly cross; the action, give and take. Kurbsky, the Russian defector, hands his sword to the king of Poland. Lounging in his royal armchair, the king takes the sword and returns it to Kurbsky, who thereby is made the liege of Poland. Next, the king produces a ribbon with a glittering cross, which he puts around Kurbsky's neck – thus making Kurbsky a knight, the king's retainer.

This is more or less what we see happening on the screen. There is, however, a slight oddity in the long shot represented in figure 8, as though Eisenstein had arranged the figures in a chessboard manner: despite the fact that the knighting ceremony is taking place at the back, those present (and the king himself) are looking off – and in the opposite direction. The thing is that, initially, Eisenstein's plan for the Polish court sequence had been more complex – or, to use his own term, more 'telescopic'. As envisaged in the scenario, in conjunction with the actual ritual there unfolds its mock version (that is what everyone is looking at), a parody within a parody, as it were, given that the knighting of Kurbsky is itself a parody of the coronation ritual shown at the beginning of Part One. This is how the scenario describes the first moments at the Polish court:

> The scene begins almost like the scene of Ivan's coronation.
> Something is happening OFF SCREEN.

Fig. 8. Knighting at the Polish court: note the chess motif.

And various groups look OFF SCREEN. […]

In the foreground
A huge white and black ball.

Clustered around it – striped jesters.
The jesters keep glancing OFF SCREEN.
And tinkle their bells.

The jesters are mimicking what is happening in the background,
As yet invisible to the spectator.

Two jesters are balancing on the ball.
One of them – the chief, browless and moonfaced – brandishes his beribboned jester's wand.
A third bends the knee before the ball.
The first dangles in front of the kneeler his wand with the ribbon, as though to invest the latter's neck with the decoration on its end.
He knocks the second jester off the ball by pushing him from behind.
The second jester falls.
A fourth jester takes a running leap over the ball.
The ball rolls.
The jesters fall in a heap one on top of the other. They freeze motionless.[28]

As shown in a drawing that Eisenstein sketched for this scene (fig. 9), the placement and movements of the 'chief jester' ordaining his counterpart into the Order of Jesters parallel those of King Sigismund beribboning Kurbsky. Even the props appear to ape each other: the jester's wand with which the mock king decorates mock Kurbsky's neck is nothing else than a puppet jester whose triple hood recalls the shape of the cross. Virtually everything about this remarkable image is charged with double meaning, including the big ball around which the whole routine pivots – a property the tongue-in-cheek symbolism of which becomes apparent as we trace Eisenstein's drawing to its source.

The clue is right before us. Beneath the drawing, we see Eisenstein's note saying: 'A plagiarism from Benois' "*ABC*." But worked so cleverly into the action, that the sin is justified.' The book in question (first published in 1905, around the time Eisenstein was learning to read)

Fig. 9 (left). Jesters and their ball: sketch for the scene not found in the film. Fig. 10 (right). Jesters and their ball: a page from the 1905 ABC by Aleksandr Benois.

is not an ordinary ABC – its designer, Alexander Benois, wanted it to do two things at once: to teach the alphabet and, in a less obvious manner, to introduce children to the vocabulary of art. This twofold purpose is also manifest in the picture from which Eisenstein borrowed his jesters and their ball (fig. 10). Technically, the picture is an acronym: the ball and the jesters stand for the words *shar* and *shuty* illustrating, respectively, the small and the capital variations of the letter 'Ш' (as 'sea' and 'stormy' might conspire to usher in the English *Ss*), but aside from the service it pays to that letter Benois' image bears a message of its own. If we take a closer look at Benois' ball, which is not merely a ball but a globe, and at his four jesters – a happy one near the top, a frightened one going downward, an angry one under the ball, and a plaintive one standing next to it – and at the king watching their antics with a thoughtful air, we will discover that what they are enacting before the king (and what Benois offers children) is an ironic version of the wheel of fortune. This was a widespread medieval emblem in which the ruler (a pathetic little figure clinging to a large wheel) is shown to go through four stages of reign: *regnabo, regno, regnavi, sum sine regno*, that is, 'I will rule, I rule, I have ruled, I am without rule.'

This mor(t)ality tale and its visual formula were still popular in

sixteenth-century Europe, both in pictures and in pageant shows where the scene would be enacted; for example, the Spanish wood engraving shown on figure 11 dates from 1552, the high tide of Ivan's reign.[29] Note the female goddess who makes the wheel turn: this image, like the whole wheel-allegory, is known to hark back to *The Consolation of Philosophy* – the book written some thousand years before by the sixth-century Roman philosopher Boethius:

> Are you trying to stay the force of her turning wheel? Ah! dull-witted mortal, if Fortune begin to stay still, she is no longer Fortune.
>
> As thus she turns her wheel of chance with haughty hand [...], fortune now tramples fiercely on a fearsome king, and now deceives no less a conquered man by raising from the ground his humbled face [...]
>
> 'I turn my wheel that spins its circle fairly; I delight to make the lowest turn to the top, the highest to the bottom. Come you to the top if you will, but on this condition, that you think it no unfairness to sink when the rule of my game demands it.'[30]

It may appear at first that the philosophical fatalism of the wheel of fortune as mimed by Eisenstein's Benois jesters has little to do with the overall story of *Ivan the Terrible* – a film whose visible narrative hinges upon the consolidation rather than the disintegration of power. However, what we see is only part of this story, two-thirds of a work mapped as a trilogy, revealing as it unfolds the price Ivan is paying for glory.

To appreciate the way Eisenstein planned to make this price known to the viewer, we need to remember 'biomechanics' – a theory (also an actors' training technique practised in left-wing theatres in the 1920s) according to which stage characters are defined by the way they move. A preparatory note (written down around the same time as Eisenstein made his Benois drawing) thus outlines a motor malfunction that overtakes Cherkasov's character as the film moves from its first part to the last:

In the first episode, Ivan's movements and changes of mood are remarkably *brisk*... In the second one they become *syncopic*... All the mobility and elan [*brosovost'*] of the first episode is reduced here to the movement of the eyes, *hauchement de la tête etc.* During the 'Last Judgment' Ivan moves as an unstrung marionette – a parody of his own self of the first episode.[31]

A remarkable thing about this project is that here the biomechanical evolution of the character is defined in the same terms that Eisenstein uses to define the development of the plot – conceived, I repeat, as a parade of parodies. First Kurbsky, then the jesters, later the poor fool Vladimir, and now – pressed against the backdrop of the doomsday fresco – Ivan himself, are shown putting on a string-puppet parody of the Tsar. Sadly, only a few stills survive from the 'Last Judgment', a scene showing Ivan's violent confession, shot for the last part of the trilogy. However, a series of sketches made in deliberately nervous strokes (figs. 12, 13, 14) also survives and gives an idea of the angular uncoordinated motions Eisenstein wanted Cherkasov to perform. Another note (penned in July 1942) specifies Ivan's behaviour afterwards:

After the 'Last Judgment': Ivan the *Stony*[32]

Fig. 12 (left). Ivan's confession: sketch for Part Three. Fig. 13 (right). Ivan's confession.

and summarises:

The 1st episode
All of him moves
The 2nd one: only his *eyes* move
Funeral feast: only his *eyelids* move,
his face and his glance are stone-like
(use adhesive tape to pull down
[Cherkasov's] lower eyelids)
Eherne Maske [an iron mask].[33]

Lastly, Naum Kleiman's theoretical reconstruction of Part Three tells us how Ivan would have looked in the finale:

"Sallow-faced," "drooping" – such were the director's instructions for the make-up and costume artists, and that is also the way he pictured Cherkasov's acting during the end sequence. We can also read it in the very figure of Ivan as depicted on Eisenstein's drawing entitled "Alone?" [fig. 15] It shows the climax of his self-destruction and the deepest point of his loneliness.[34]

Despite the inevitable fluidity of Eisenstein's work-in-progress, we can count up to six transformations (particularly striking since other characters remain ageless) that mark Ivan's itinerary from hope to let-down – a cycle also described by the wheel of fortune whose spinning the jesters' ball conveys so well. One may even go as far as to speculate why exactly Eisenstein thought his little plagiarism so clever: the task behind the act we see Benois' clowns perform before the king – to remind the ruler of the sad trajectory of rule – was, in a sense, identical to his own. This theory, of course, cannot be proved or disproved, but whether or not Eisenstein perceived his aim this way, Stalin must have: only the first (ascending) part of the story was allowed to come to the screen at the time as the 'main spectator' (as they used to whisper in the

1940s) was still alive. Part Two was banned, Part Three left unfinished.

Let me add that Benois' image is not to be taken as a clue to a direct allegorical reading of the film – not even if it were included in the final version. Allegory may help to explain the workings of power, but it tells us nothing about the workings of Eisenstein's film. In effect, the way this film works – and the kind of reading it asks for – is contrary to allegory. Central among the film's mechanisms is a safety device averting direct readings, be they political, historical or moral. Earlier on in his career Eisenstein used to call this device 'conflict' or 'collision', and by the time he made *Ivan* preferred 'dialectical struggle of opposites'. Alive throughout his work, however, there was a conviction that the true task of an artist was not to shape or educate, but to confuse and jolt viewers out of their comfortably consistent picture of the world.

The Montage-image
It may sound paradoxical, but in Eisenstein's art theory the smallest indivisible unit always consists of two things, not one. What constitutes the structure of the work is for him not A or B, but the difference, the tension growing between them in their twin cell – until the *nux* outgrows the nutshell (a little organic explosion) only to reproduce the contradiction on a higher level. Speaking of film, Eisenstein dubbed such a unit a 'montage-image' (*montazhnyi obraz*). As distinct from

images as representations, Eisenstein's montage-image harbours mutually conflicting features.

The montage-image is not only about montage. Acting, lighting, art design – in *Ivan*, any aspect of film-making may be found to embody the principle of internal contradiction. Consider a grand mural that covers the walls and the ceiling of the reception hall – the space of anger and mercy, used in the film (as in real life) to announce decrees and receive foreign embassies. A miniature from an old chronograph that depicts one such ceremony in amazing detail (fig. 16; note the

Fig. 16 (right). Sixteenth-century miniature depicting Ivan's Reception Chamber.

Fig. 17 (left). Ivan's Reception Chamber as shown in Part Two.

throne, the figures seated along the side walls and the entrance wall shown only in part in order not to block the people behind it) tells nothing about any paintings on its walls or ceiling; evidently, the chronicler was more interested in the event than in the room.[35]

Eisenstein, who knew this miniature, remains reasonably faithful to this source for the architecture and seating arrangement – he even preserves its peculiar sense of perspective down the hall – but adds a big

mural of his own. (We happen to know that Eisenstein was very pleased with this choice – one of his working notes reads: 'The angel figure in the reception chamber is the best graphic image I have so far managed to produce – made on March 30, 1942.'[36]) The mural shows rolling clouds along the sides (a recurrence of the thundercloud-motif planted in the credits), and, all along the ceiling above the clouds, the Angel of Apocalypse with scales in his right hand and a sinuous sword in his left.[37] The sun-like face of the angel extends beyond the space of the ceiling and appears hanging upside down from the wall over the entrance (fig. 17). This, however, is only part of the angel

Fig. 18. The angel mural: ceiling and two walls shown in a blueprint projection.

Fig. 19. The image behind the throne: the angel's feet trampling the face of the Universe.

Fig. 20. The image over the entrance: the angel's flaming face staring from above.

Fig. 21. Conflict of powers: the mural as 'visual commentary'.

figure; the whole of it, as seen in the sketch Eisenstein made (fig. 18), probably to explain this idea to the set decorator Iosif Shpinel, can only be shown in orthogonal projection since the feet of the angel – shown trampling the face of the Universe[38] – fold over the wall behind the throne (fig. 19). Twice-folded, Eisenstein's angel of wrath turns literally into a montage-image – the image impossible to take in at a glance – and also, if one may say so, into a 'surround icon', an icon impossible to escape.

I leave to the viewer the joy of discovering how these two images – the face radiating flames and the face being trodden down – placed, vis-à-vis, on opposite walls yet parts of the same image, are made to participate in the confrontation that takes place between Ivan and Philip Kolychev in Part Two (figs 20 and 21). Let me only mention a visual rhyme I might have passed by were it not for a piece of paper on which Eisenstein sketched two

Fig. 22. Young Ivan reaches out for a foothold.

Fig. 23. Young Ivan under his regents' control: note the feet above his head.

shots storyboarding the prologue – a sequence which, shortly before the release of Part One, Eisenstein was forced to shift to Part Two where it figures as a flashback.

Ivan tells Kolychev (another friend-turned-opponent, the same Kolychev who together with Kurbsky was pouring gold on Ivan in Part One) why he hates boyars: they killed his mother and humiliated him as a child. Fade-in; black, smoking clouds; the last glimpse of the poisoned mother; then, there follows a scene showing two grotesque boyars, thick and thin, misruling in his name while little Ivan is shown sitting on the throne, his foot groping vainly for a foothold (fig. 22). This foot, Eisenstein comments, echoes the foot of the angel seen behind the boy's head in an earlier shot (fig. 23)[39] – which explains why we see these two shots juxtaposed in his preparatory drawing (fig. 24). A system of cross-references is thereby created: foot-foot, foot-face, lack of power, excess of power. This is what Eisenstein had in mind when speaking of the montage-image.

We need Eisenstein to help us read *Ivan the Terrible* because in the film Eisenstein's theory and practice form a vicious circle; unlocking it risks trivialising both the film and the theory. Would many of us be able to see a connection between the foot of a fresco figure visible in shot A and the foot of a film character shown in shot B, or construe, at a viewing, all the avatars

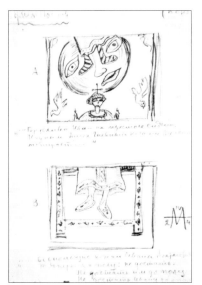

of the cloud motif unless prompted by Eisenstein's notes? I doubt it – not because our perceptiveness or visual memory is below Eisenstein's (perhaps; but isn't this also what makes us admire Joyce or Picasso?), but because, for better or for worse, we simply do not watch movies the way Eisenstein thought – or, at his low moments, wished – we did.

We ought to try to meet him halfway. Not only Eisenstein's vision of things, but also his image of himself, were predicated on the paradox of indivisible duality, a feature which Eisenstein, this incorrigible self-observer, thought indispensable

Fig. 24. Sketch with a comment on the 'visual rhyme' between two shots (figs. 22-23.)   33

for his work to take off from the ground: 'My activity: one wing – analytical, another – imagery.'[40] In this sense, Eisenstein *is* a montage-image: the physical body of his film (I am not toying with the occult, it is just a way of saying it) has an invisible twin – the mental movie without which the first is not complete.

Images on Walls

The difference between the way we watch films and the way he wanted us to begins at the level of cognitive habits. 'Make it absolutely compulsory for *sinister* scenes' (1942);[41] 'Painted background as an emotional commentary to dramatis personae – this principle must become key as to the staging' (1941)[42] – these notes, as well as two or three similar entries from Eisenstein's working journal, document his pledge to treat elements of set design on a par with film characters. The idea was highly unusual – not only did it defy the intrinsic tendency of the eye to separate the figure from the foil, but it also went against a basic viewing habit: as film viewers, we are not used to inspecting walls – we take them for granted.

Consider Archbishop Pimen – an example that allows us to trace, step by step, the way Eisenstein makes a film character unfold and merge ('*wholly*' or '*almost* wholly') with the surrounding space. Stage one: early on, Eisenstein wants Pimen (a major force behind the conspiracy) to be associated with death: 'Pimen is all white […] His face is almost a cranium:

yellow and white. Pearl embroidery.'[43] Stage two: sketching the make-up scheme for Vsevolod Pudovkin (initially supposed to play Pimen), Eisenstein adds a skull-like quality to his head (fig. 25). Throughout stages three and four, we find him apply the same idea to the set design. Planning a scene in which Pimen demands that Philip bring the Tsar to his heels, Eisenstein sketched a room of dark vaults covered with white frescos (fig. 26); pinned onto the sketch are two photographic reproductions of genuine frescos (taken from a 1941 book on Russian monumental painting[44]),

Fig. 25. Make-up sketch for Pimen (to be played by Vsevolod Pudovkin).

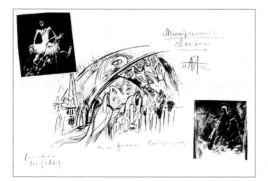

Fig. 27 (below left). The Doomsday Angel. Fig. 28 (below right). The Doomsday Horseman.

one featuring the doomsday angel with bird-like wings (fig. 27), another the apocalyptic horseman with a skull for a head (fig. 28), each to be enlarged to fill the vaults.

Finally, stage five, the phase of staging: Eisenstein manoeuvres Aleksandr Mgebrov (who now plays Pimen) in such a way that the dead head of the apocalyptic horseman – an 'emotional commentary' – appears behind the archbishop looking almost like his white shadow, or, as it were, his peripheral self (fig. 29).

We may note, following Kristin Thompson, a partial overlapping: Pimen's crosier seems to form a scythe for the skeleton.[45] As Eisenstein moves Pimen towards Philip, the two seem gradually to merge – this time, 'wholly' – with the other fresco, the doomsday angel, one of the wings of which now appears to be growing from the character's body (fig. 30).

Fig. 29. Pimen 'echoed' by the Doomsday Horseman figure on the wall behind.

Fig. 30. Pimen 'merged' with the Doomsday Angel on the wall behind.

In this respect, *Ivan the Terrible* is only relatively a movie: Eisenstein casts his viewer as a beholder looking (not watching!) at a painting by an old master, eye-primed for allegories, emblems and visual rhymes. However, I do not want to mislead the reader into taking this statement too literally. *Ivan the Terrible* is not an attempt to escape from cinema to painting, or to smuggle paintings into films. Regardless of his stake in art, Eisenstein saw his work on *Ivan* as quintessentially cinematic – as opposed to the work of some others, whose vaunted realism he dismissed as stock pictorialism. This is what his 1942 working diary says about Vladimir Petrov's two-part film, *Peter the First* (1937–39) – a favourite of Stalin's, the type of biopic that Eisenstein knew he too was expected to turn out: 'Acting in Petrov's film is a *succession* of <u>poses</u>. Equally, there is no montage but merely a succession of easel-painting shots. And the scenario is not an organism, but a checklist of *traits*.'[46]

Ivan the Terrible

The primary aim of this self-addressed note was not so much to critique *Peter the First* as to characterise the problem Eisenstein wanted his Ivan to evade: unlike Petrov's Peter, Eisenstein's hero was to embrace mutually exclusive rather than mutually complementary character traits. This is what he means by writing 'there is no montage'. Eisenstein conceived of *Ivan the Terrible* as a montage-image – what matters is not what we see at any given moment, but how what we are seeing now relates to what we have seen a moment ago: in other words, our response to contradictory clues.

To put this idea into practice, Eisenstein devised a number of strategies, some of which I would like to discuss below. Let me begin with a relatively simple case: Ivan's joke I quoted in the plot summary about falling bells and empty heads, which the Tsar makes at the beginning of Part One as he confronts the rebellious mob that has broken into the palace. The joke, made as everyone apprehends a punishment, wins Ivan instant popularity (with the crowd as with the viewers). Yet, at once, Eisenstein makes him cap this with another, somewhat more sinister joke which foreshadows the atrocities to come in Part Two: 'And can a head fall off … all by itself? In order to fall, it has to be cut …'

Now consider the lighting of this scene. Figures 31 and 32, two sample frames from the same shot, with only a moment or two separating one from the other, show Ivan's face before and after the word 'cut' (reinforced by the gesture): before, the face appears evenly lit (fig. 31), one could almost say flatly, were it not for the fact that this 'flatness' serves to offset a sudden shadow that hits the face as soon as the word is out (fig. 32). This abrupt shift is not the only thing that happens. Those of my readers within reach of a DVD player will be rewarded to observe how this montage-image is reinforced by a musical accent.

I have called this case simple because such universally understood metaphors as light and shadow hardly need to be explained. It was not Eisenstein's way, however, to content himself with simple things, no matter how powerful. Figures 33 and 34 illustrate an apparently similar device – another sudden change in the lighting scheme aimed to create, within the space of one shot, a conflict-laden montage-image. It happens in Part Two: in the middle of the flashback, the storyline re-emerges for a moment in the present to show the Tsar relating the sad story of his childhood. Here the contrast does not rely so much upon our primal response to light and shadow, but depends on different degrees of softness and on the directionality of light – and on the way in which Eisenstein foreshortens Cherkasov's face. It is the same shot, I repeat, but

Fig. 31. Ivan before the joke.

Fig. 32. Ivan after the joke.

its two ends are charges with polar energies. It begins in diffused penumbra (fig. 33) – Ivan remembers his mother and ends in hard-edged chiaroscuro (fig. 34) – Ivan remembers who killed her. Calm backlighting; a distant spotlight adds a sentimental lustre to Ivan's eyes; and the comely three-quarter angle is intended to give Ivan a Christ-like tinge. Then, a sudden swing of the head makes the facial angle disquieting and the stare maniacal, while the light, like a flash of lightning, strikes the face from below – a lighting scheme the likes of which we tend to associate with things Satanic.

The idea is clear – the character of Ivan cannot be taken in at a glance. Was this idea cinematic? For Eisenstein it was, but hardly for us – for whom the word spells compliance with the norm. Take the above examples. Seen separately, any of these lighting set-ups is but a stock item of photographic vocabulary. Yet the way Eisenstein shifted them around –

Fig. 33. Ivan remembers his mother.

Fig. 34. Ivan recalls who killed her.

with the dauntless disregard for realistic motivation he had admired on the Kabuki stage – tips his idiom towards the fringe of the commonly accepted.

Or take Ivan's make-up. In *Non-Indifferent Nature* Eisenstein describes the formidable task he had given the make-up artist Vasilii Goriunov: to make of Cherkasov's face a kaleidoscope of fleeting resemblances without ever letting the viewer pin any of them down – from the biblical villain Nebuchadnezzar to the righteous Jew, Uriel Acosta (of the eponymous tragedy by Karl Gutzkov), from (Leonardo's?) Judas and the conventional stage Mephistopheles to the Jesus Christ of Christian iconography.[47] Indeed, one recognises some conventional traits of Mephisto – broken eyebrows and the V-shaped piece ('widow's peak'[48]) wedging into the middle of his forehead – particularly if a picture of Ivan is placed next to a 'Devil' diagram which, for the sake of comparison, I borrowed from the old make-up manual by Serge Strenkovsky[49] (fig. 35).

Looking at these pictures, it is not easy to imagine how Eisenstein could have possibly hoped to make this face correspond with the image of Christ. But let me examine one case in which such resemblance is indeed conjured up – through allusions to art. It happens in Part One, when we find Ivan either mortally ill or pretending to be so – in any case, he miraculously resurrects himself to reward his true friends and to make note of would-be dissenters. Consider a self-addressed memo complete with two sketches which Eisenstein jotted down to show the position of Cherkasov's head in a scene showing Ivan unconscious (fig. 36). The Russian text reads: 'Ivan's illness. To attain the "Holbein effect", *put the head not on a pillow*, but flatly, aligned with the body.' The reference (repeated, in English, above the sketch at the bottom – 'Note this in Holbein') is to *The Body of the Dead Christ in the Tomb*, the sixteenth-century painting by Hans Holbein.

To trace the way Eisenstein works Holbein's picture into the film, compare Christ's detail (fig. 37) with the sketch and the resulting movie. In the sketch (fig. 36), the head appears in two foreshortenings – the three-quarter variation replicates Holbein's; the other (the strict profile) is Eisenstein's own. These are not, as it may appear, two studies for one shot: both the profile and the 'Holbein' three-quarter appear in the actual movie (figs. 38 and 39). Eisenstein, as it were, 'cuts into' Holbein's picture,

Fig. 35 (left). Mephisto make-up: instructional drawing. Fig. 36 (right). Ivan's illness: studies of head positions.

dividing his image in two. In both, we should add, Ivan's beard is shown sticking out – in the unnatural manner condemned by Stalin's men.

Nor is this all. Between the 'Holbein' close-up and its profile variation Eisenstein spliced a shot that taps another source of Christian iconography. The manner in which Anastasia touches Ivan's foot (fig. 40) evokes Magdalene lamenting Christ as she is usually shown in *pietà* compositions – for example, this Magdalene in a *pietà* by Sandro

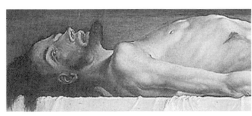

Fig. 37. Hans Holbein the Younger, *The Body of the Dead Christ in the Tomb* (1521). Detail.

Fig. 38. Head position (cf. fig. 36, upper study).

Fig. 39. The 'Holbein' head position (figs 37 and 36, bottom).

Fig. 40. Anastasia at Ivan's feet.

Fig. 41. Magdalene at Christ's feet: Alessandro Botticelli, *Lamentation over the Dead Christ with the Saints Jerome, Paul and Peter* (c. 1490). Detail.

Botticelli recalls Anastasia not only in attitude but even in the way her arm locks in a continuous curve with the foot and leg of Christ (fig. 41).

This example explains why Eisenstein considered his approach quintessentially cinematic – despite the fact that *Ivan* draws upon the art of painting more than it draws from life. Eisenstein used to call his aesthetics 'operational'[50] – and, indeed, the way *Ivan* taps the artistic tradition looks more like a cinematic operation than a pictorialist sponging of the sort he found at work in Petrov's *Peter*. Eisenstein evokes Holbein not because he wants *Ivan* to *look* like pictures, but to make Holbein *work* for *Ivan*, and work the way only films are meant to work – by controlling the viewer's associations. For it was Eisenstein's old theory, still alive from the times when he, like virtually every Soviet film-maker of the early 1920s, was carried away with Pavlov's teaching about the working of human and animal brains. The theory held that by showing this or that thing, e.g. a calf being slaughtered in *Strike*, the film director could arouse in the viewer this or that 'unconditioned reflex' and deflect the ensuing emotion onto something else, e.g. onto the police shown raiding the strikers' quarters. In principle, *Ivan* works the same way, the only difference being that in his early films Eisenstein preferred to work with physiological stimuli, whereas in *Ivan* he counts on our responses to culture.

Shadows

I hope it will not sound too philosophical if I say that, in defiance of the mental habit that makes us think of the soul as something residing 'inside' the body, the 'inner' – that is, essential – character in *Ivan* is seldom confined to the shell of its physical self. In some cases, as we have just seen, the actor's physical body may house a host of characters; in some others, there is not enough room for one – the character becomes a compound equation that involves both the figure and the surrounding space: a fresco, a shadow.

Once again, I am impelled to refer to the meeting between Eisenstein and Stalin, during which that Kremlin ideologist, Andrei Zhdanov, made the remarks about Ivan's beard sticking up in an unnatural manner and about Eisenstein's obtrusive shadows allegedly distracting the viewer from the action. This section is about Eisenstein's shadows, but before we turn to those, let me quote another opinion, which seems almost to echo Zhdanov's, but which comes from a source that could not be more remote from the Kremlin. The strangeness of Ivan's beard caught the eye of a much worthier critic, the American director Orson Welles (one of Eisenstein's favourites), who was both impressed and taken aback by what he called 'Eisenstein's uninhibited preoccupation with pictorial effect'. Let me quote a witticism from Welles' 1945 review of *Ivan* which will be better appreciated by those who remember that the hammer and sickle were two symbols interlocked in the Soviet state emblem:

> What's wrong with [the film], when it's wrong, is what goes sour in the work of any artist whose bent is for eloquence. The Tsar's beard, for instance, cutting like a mighty sickle through the hammer blows of the drama, isn't nearly as entertaining to the audience as it was to the director.[51]

And I am almost sure I know the shot that fuelled this hammer-and-sickle joke – it must be the scene in which Eisenstein makes Cherkasov toss back

Fig. 42. Ivan's beard forms
a cross with a candle
behind it.

his head so that his beard intersects with the candle behind it to suggest the shape of a cross (fig. 42).

So much for the beard; apart from the Holbein Christ reference there is little of relevance to be found in Eisenstein's notes that explains its defiant curve. We are more fortunate with respect to the shadows – the other source of Zhdanov's discontent – and what Eisenstein wanted them to mean. In the introduction to this book I quoted Eisenstein's diary entry of 20 October 1946, in which he claims that if *Ivan* looks 'overburdened' with shadows, then it is only to those whose interest in films starts and ends with the story. This entry does not stop here – Eisenstein also explains how he intended some of these shadows to work. To do so, he diagrammed by hand three shots from the scene that takes place in the stateroom (that is, the study in which Ivan is shown instructing his envoy

Fig. 43. Shadow one:
Ivan's 'stately mind'.

to Britain). He even supplied these with captions which tell that the enormous profile cast onto the wall behind (fig. 43) suggests the dimension of statesmanship or, literally, Ivan's 'stately mind' (*gosudarstvennyi um*),[52] whereas the shadow of the astrolabe above Ivan's head (fig. 44) reflects '*a maze of his cosmic world thoughts*'[53] (this in English). We also learn that the 'shadow theatre' displayed on the wall behind Ivan as he gives instructions to the envoy (fig. 45) is governed by the same logic that makes pharaohs appear large and slaves small in Egyptian sepulchral art: 'The disproportion of two shadows reflects the genuine difference of scales between two characters which normally would appear identically dimensioned.'[54]

In other words, Ivan's 'outer ego' projected – literally – onto the wall behind him works to conjure up his truer – non-material, non-physical –

Fig. 44. Shadow two: '*a maze of his cosmic world thoughts*'.

Fig. 45. Shadow three: 'the difference of scales between two characters'.

self, much as the skull we see looming behind Pimen's back (fig. 29) served to append apocalyptic associations to the character of the archbishop. There exists one sense, though, in which the operation with shadows differs from the method of associations-through-culture to which I referred in the previous section. Shadows not only emancipated the film director from the drab, inert, stolid 'dimension' of physical reality, letting him scale up the significant at will (the freedom that Eisenstein equally admired in children's art and the art of the ancients); they also allowed him to depict the ineffable – in his favourite way, for shadows also belong to the world of 'primitive thinking' which *Ivan the Terrible* (or, according to Eisenstein, any artwork) invokes. Another diary entry (made on the same day) goes on to link the peculiar two-tiered structure of the stateroom sequence to the assumed shadow cult of the past:

> The dual reading of the figure and its shadow [in *Ivan* must be seen] *als Auswuchs* [as an outgrowth] of the primal mental concept positing *the autonomy of each*. Here, as there, we face the 'autonomy' of meanings pertaining, in this sense, to different 'worlds', or *dimensions* – an *Auswuchs* based on the mythological stage [of mentality], and therefore drawing upon its [emotional] *appeal!* [Last word in English].[55]

As he writes this, Eisenstein suddenly discovers an unlikely (hence all the more exciting) comedic parallel that (if one may say so about parallels) meets *Ivan* in the plane of this mythological past:

> In one American musical (possibly, with Shirley Temple[56]) a black dancer is shown dancing against the background of a giant shadow. Next thing we see is that the shadow ceases to repeat his movements and starts dancing the dance of its own (a shadow dancing in a counterpoint duo with its own source!)[57]

This detour is less fortuitous than it seems. In his writings, Eisenstein often bemoans the fact that the film genre he was working in deprived him of the freedom enjoyed by eccentrics and animators who, much like children and the ancients, had the licence to pay no heed whatsoever to reality. In the perceptive review of *Ivan* already quoted, Orson Welles spotted this comedic element that underlies Eisenstein's conception of visual style: 'Critics and audiences in the English-speaking world, accustomed as they are to the pallid stylelessness of the "realistic" school, are likely to be impatient, even moved to giggles by the antics of Ivan and his friends.'[58]

This is not confined to the English-speaking world alone, as we can judge from Zhdanov's criticism: cinematic 'realism' was everyman's taste; anything else was prone to seem ridiculous. The risk Eisenstein took of not conforming to it was his conscious choice. If I were asked to define the genre of *Ivan the Terrible* – a film so determined to dodge all generic conventions – I would suggest that it should carry the name of 'eccentric tragedy'.

Eccentric Tragedy

To justify this apparent oxymoron, let me dwell upon another of Eisenstein's paradoxical confessions, even if this time a little more patience might be required to explore the maze of Eisenstein's thought – which, indeed, is nothing short of 'cosmic'. Once again, I will cite a note from Eisenstein's diary (April 1942) which puts his current work on *Ivan* in a context so strange that, to be helpful, it must in its turn be put in the context of what Eisenstein had been reading and thinking about in the span of five years or so. The note begins with a parallel (which is anything but obvious) between *Ivan* and *The Battleship Potemkin* (made some seventeen years earlier); then, by an association less whimsical than it may look, leaps to Shakespeare, and, of all people, to Charlie Chaplin, the eccentric comedian much favoured by Eisenstein. Here is, with a few omissions, the rather puzzling passage:

> *Pot[emkin]* is absolutely [*Ivan*] *Grozny en miniature*, i.e. the principle of its montage structure is absolutely the same as the scenario *macrostructure* [of *Ivan*]! [...] The body of regal power here – and the body of the rebel vessel there! (Funny – 'Down with the autocracy' there – and its exact opposite here!) [...] The battleship (here, the Tsar) like the human body, consists of co-members [*razvernut, kak chelovek, na sochleny*]. The co-members – hands, feet, head – live in conflict, [but] within the unity of the theme, they add up to it. Calls to mind the passage from Shakespeare's *Coriolanus* with its conflict between the organs of the body.

> And, via this passage, I (for the first time) determine the link: montage – the movement of human [body] – *par excellence*, the *movement* and *behavior* of Chaplin.

> The eccentric breaks up into pieces the habitual mechanism of organic movement, re-linking them arbitrarily through montage.

[…] The way the arm and the leg, the torso and the extremities correlate in their common movement *is not the same* – the way they are *linked up*, or inter-conditioned is different from the way they are in normal organic movement.

To explain what part this unlikely community of names – Potemkin, Coriolanus, Chaplin – played in the building of Ivan (the character then still in scaffolding), let me refer to two books – one English, another German – which helped to shape Eisenstein's idea of tragedy.

The English one was *Shakespeare's Imagery and What It Tells Us*, the monograph by Caroline Spurgeon which someone in London (most probably, Ivor Montagu) had sent to Eisenstein in November 1935. What Spurgeon's *Shakespeare's Imagery* told Eisenstein (to be guided by marginal notes in the copy found at Eisenstein's memorial apartment in Moscow and the sales receipt from 'John and Edward Bumbrus' slipped into it as a bookmark) was the central role of body metaphors in Shakespeare's tragedies. Eisenstein became particularly interested in those which, in his eyes, condensed, in a nutshell, the germ, the reason, the mainspring of tragedy at large: images of dismemberment in *King Lear*, the tragedy of divided land, and the allegory of – may we say so? – socio-somatic disorder, like the one that Menenius, the patrician in *Coriolanus* throws in the face of the rebellious crowd (the trope, Spurgeon writes, had been taken over by Shakespeare wholesale from North's *Plutarch*[59]):

There was a time when all the body's members,
Rebelled against the belly, thus accused it:
That only like a gulf it did remain
I' th' midst o' th' body, idle and unactive,
Still cupboarding the viand, never bearing
Like labour with the rest; where the other instruments
Did see and hear, devise, instruct, walk, feel,
And, mutually participate, did minister
Unto the appetite and affection common
Of the whole body. The belly answered—[60]

I abstain from quoting more in order not to mislead the reader into thinking that Eisenstein, this rebel to the marrow of his bones, could, for a moment, sympathise with the sated wisdom of the belly's answer. His interest points elsewhere. What Eisenstein found exciting about Spurgeon's monograph was that her close-to-text observations confirmed, to him, a more universal theory of tragedy he not only subscribed to, but even tried to develop – matching it up with the theory of film montage as laid out in his extensive study *Montage 1937*.

Which brings us to that other – German – book that proved crucial for the making of *Ivan: The Origin of Tragedy. A Psychoanalytical Essay on the History of Greek Tragedy* published by Freudian psychologist Alfred Winterstein in 1925.[61] The thing that struck Eisenstein about this study – or, rather, this Freudian rereading of an idea proposed by British classical scholar Gilbert Murray – was Winterstein's point that tragedy replays (and, thus, revives in our subliminal mind) the ritual killing of the king – a primordial rite whereby the community members were believed to tear into pieces the body of the leader before eating it together as a symbolic act meant to ascertain that the leader's body was now one with the higher body, the body of the collective.

I hasten to add, before I am interrupted, that my reference to tragedy stands in direct connection with Eisenstein's theories. Even though it was to end up with the hero alive, Eisenstein refused to call the *Ivan* trilogy anything but tragedy. Early on – well before he ran across Winterstein's *Origin of Tragedy* – Eisenstein had observed that, by its very technical nature, film-making involves two operations that mirror each other: at the stage of production the director fragments 'reality' into shots only to reassemble them, in a different manner, on the editing table – the break-and-make process which he liked to compare to the way the Japanese juggle with simple pictures to form compound hieroglyphs. Winterstein's view of tragedy gave Eisenstein's theory of montage a new, more powerful analogy: he now discovered that the two mirror operations inscribed in the work of tragedy and the technique of film-making were essentially the same, since (according to Winterstein) the tragic hero goes through the stage of *sparagmos* – being torn to pieces – on the way to resurrection, or apotheosis. Moreover, *in embryo*, this cycle (dismembering–reassembling) was said to stem from the cannibalistic ritual intended to fuse, by fission, the individual body and the collective – to transform private into social. Ergo, montage carries the seed of tragedy, and, conversely, tragedy is a historical form of montage.

Viewed in the perspective of these books, the underlying site of a true tragedy, regardless of its setting, is the human body (hence the equation between 'the body of the rebel vessel' in *Potemkin* and 'the body of regal power' in *Ivan*); while its ultimate action – the act of dismemberment and subsequent welding – is montage. Given that, for Eisenstein, 'montage' meant 'conflict', it will now be easier to account for the mental curve that had led him from there to Shakespeare, and from Shakespeare to Chaplin. From ancient times, says *Montage 1937*, art has known the secret of the 'Osiris method' (here Eisenstein evokes the Egyptian god deemed to relive, seasonally, dismemberment and resurrection) – the precarious equilibrium (or, better, the dynamic tension) between unity and disunity, the centrifugal and centripetal.[62] For Eisenstein, the image of the body organs risen against each other was not therefore a mere didactic parable of a dysfunctional rule of the kind depicted in *Coriolanus*, but rather a meta-image of tragedy as a genre, Shakespeare's insight into the hidden mechanism of tragedy; hence that phrase in the diary entry under discussion: 'the co-members – hands, feet, head – live in conflict, [but] within the unity of the theme, they add up to it.'

This is where the notion of eccentricity comes in. Imagine how nonplussed an established dramatic actor would be to hear Eisenstein directing him to depict a character whose hands, feet and head 'live in conflict' with each other. There is, therefore, little wonder that the only type of performer that Eisenstein thought fit for the role of Ivan would be an eccentric comedian: ideally Charlie Chaplin, but realistically Nikolai Cherkasov, a virtuoso comedy actor whose musichall numbers Eisenstein had admired – exactly for this actor's ability to make his (incredibly long) limbs live their own life:

> [In the eccentric actor] the way the arm and the leg, the torso and the extremities correlate in their common movement *is not the same* – the way they are *linked up*, or inter-conditioned is different from the way they are in normal organic movement.

To return to Eisenstein's *Ivan* as an actual movie (as distinct from a diary movie, the virtual *Ivan* addressed so far in this chapter), how does all this reading and thinking relate to what we can see and hear on the screen? First, there are various thematic echoes, like that 'Osiris body' metaphor in Ivan's coronation speech used to justify Russia's military claim on northern and southern seas:

> Our native land is no more than a trunk whose limbs have been hacked off at the knees and elbows. The sources of our waterways and rivers – Volga, Dvina, Bolkhovo – are ours; but the ports at their mouths are in foreign hands.

An inquisitive viewer will find more of those; of greater moment, however, than mere thematic references or political rhetoric, was Eisenstein's belief in three things. First, if he wanted *Ivan* to work as a tragedy, he needed to think of the film not so much as a 'text', not in terms of its being a story 'about' a hero, but as a 'body' – a structural counterpart of the hero's body (of the kinds Spurgeon finds hidden in Shakespeare's imagery). Second (and this comes from Murray via Winterstein) the body of the hero and that of the film must be an 'eccentric' body, a torn-apart structure constantly reassembling. Third – and this, if I am not mistaken, was Eisenstein's original contribution – there must be a dynamic, a back-and-forth interaction between the eccentric body of the actor and the eccentric body of the film.

Let me explain what it means and what visual corollary this concept has for the film. 'Eccentric' means – says Eisenstein – ex-central, ex-static. The character 'explodes' to expand – Eisenstein used to call this *vykhod iz sebia*, 'coming out of oneself'. The montage-image – the duality, the contradiction – 'planted' inside the hero's physical body transcends it in order to be reproduced, as we have seen, in the double play of the body and the shadow, or of the body and the fresco. The expansion does not stop at that. To revert to Eisenstein's vocabulary (spiced, after 1945, with bits and pieces of nuclear physics), art is an atom bomb – its fission chain leads to the '*dissolution* of matter' [italics for English].[63] Alongside corporeal heroes, writes Eisenstein, Shakespeare's tragedy conceals an unnamed one, dissolved, as it were, in textual images of the body;[64] by the same token, no effort after Eisenstein's understanding of Ivan will bear fruit as long as it is focused on Ivan as a hero. Ivan is not just the character in the film – the man *is* the film.

Twinning

The textual presence – indeed, pan-textual omnipresence – of Ivan shows, first of all, on his fellow characters, conceived as various refractions of his self. In other words, *Ivan* is a monodrama, or, as Eisenstein defined his film, it is 'the dramatic form growing out from the inner monologue [of the hero]'.[65] In the final analysis, the world of the film is that of Ivan; other characters are but extensions of his image.

The method that Eisenstein stuck to in 'growing' the system of characters from the central one was what he calls *dédoublement*:[66] making film characters propagate by twinning. Take Ivan and his friend-turned-foe Kurbsky; look at the shot showing their profiles that look like one face

Fig. 46. Twin profiles.

lobed into two, identical by contrast (fig. 46); compare this visual statement to two memos written in February and April 1942 – at the time when *Ivan*'s system of character was in a nascent state:

> Kurbsky is the negative of Ivan: fair hair, blue eyes, and very much *Jean en beau* in his clever and characteristic face.[67]
>
> Ivan is the sun; Kurbsky is the moon (this should become clear from armor emblems on their breasts). Find a place for a line: the moon only shines with reflected light (was it known already?). Give this line to Kurbsky – if it was known already – they did have globes at that time, didn't they?[68]

Let me take a look at another member of Ivan's environment, the notorious hangman Maliuta Skuratov, a character that gave Eisenstein plenty of trouble. Ivan's era, let's recall, held a special status for Stalin: depicting it was like holding the mirror up to his own. From the outset, Eisenstein feared that the slightest ambivalence in his treatment of Ivan's epoch (which, for him, was the whole point of working on the film) might be stifled by anyone appointed to evaluate his script. This is, for instance, how his diary reacts to the suggestion to cut down on the number of executions found in the internal review by professor Militsa Nechkina, the acknowledged expert on Russian history: 'This is exactly the remark *from above* I am very afraid of. If I agree, the film will lose "the bared teeth of the epoch (*of both!*)" [the last word in English].'[69]

In avoiding this fate, Maliuta was Eisenstein's main hope – a character upon whom to shift the bulk of the blame. The balance was anything but simple to find. Aside from his natural dislike of standard solutions, there was a political reason why Eisenstein could not make Maliuta the absolute villain we find him to be in most novels, plays and films, and, as far as I am concerned, he may as well have been in real history: the Tsar needed a link with the people. Initially, to serve this purpose, Eisenstein had drafted a duo of Chokhov brothers, two cheerful cannoneers (who even talked in rhyme with each other!) But he was told 'from above' that their folksy humour smacked of buffoonery, and had to cross the Chokhovs out. This explains why, despite the fact that the historical Maliuta came from noble kin, Eisenstein's was made a commoner – which, of course, made him a meagre sort of villain.

In addition, even if, by demonising Maliuta, Eisenstein had succeeded in showing 'the bare teeth of the epoch', the treasured ambivalence of Ivan would accordingly subside. Polarised characters would turn *Ivan* into a melodrama – what Eisenstein was looking for was *dédoublement*: like Ivan, though at a different level, Maliuta had to be made fearsome and likeable all at once.

> 10 III 42
> Agonisingly [I] search for the middle link for Maliuta. And it seems I have found it. Confer Chokhovs' scenes to Maliuta!!! *Great*! […] [B]rilliant: a *merry hangman*!!! And, in addition, a monumental one. By the way, it will make even funnier his disgrace at the Staritsky's house. Hurrah! Hurrah! Hurrah![70]

> Excellent: Maliuta is the class-mate [*odnoklassnik* – the pun on 'belonging to the same class' – *Y. T.*] of Chokhovs. Close to peasants. The boor's heel [*piata khama*] on the boyar's neck. And, as a result, Ivan is *nowhere* directly involved in the bloody dirt – in the menial work of blood![71]

> […] *c'est un coup de génie* – to solve all the scenes of reprisal through humour. Only the first execution […] and the final one, the end of [Vladimir and Efrosinia] Staritsky are *tragique*. The rest [of the executions] must be served with dense Rabelaisian humor. Chisel *shifts* and twists from funny to horrible moments.[72]

Making Maliuta a cannoneer and a demolition expert gained Eisenstein, at one strike, a number of points – some serious, some 'Rabelaisian'. First, according to war historians, it was Ivan's trust in guns and powder that won him the battle over Kazan, so it made sense for Eisenstein to make the Tsar's first associate the man of modern warfare – an issue whose topicality in the post-war climate we can guess from a biased but perceptive 1947 review by the American critic James Agee:

> [Eisenstein] seems all but desperately absorbed in communicating political ideas and vindications, especially parallels to Stalin and his regime. Ivan's siege and defeat of Kazan, to choose one of the simpler examples, becomes an interesting text on dealing with a foreign enemy: while the enemy watches the army which threaten their walls, you tunnel beneath their city, roll in kegs of gunpowder, and blow it to kingdom come, meaning *your* kingdom [italics in the original].[73]

Secondly, making Maliuta a sapper – 'the man of black powder and earth'[74] – enabled Eisenstein to find him a place within the body of power that is symmetrically – one could almost say geometrically – opposed to that of Kurbsky, the man of panache and the believer in the old-fashioned cavalry charge. Functional under the walls of Kazan, this specialisation acquires a symbolic dimension as the film unfolds. Maliuta is a mole – both as the sapper he had been earlier, and later, in Part Two, as the mastermind of Ivan's secret police. The first – 1941 – version of the literary treatment even contained the 'parable of two candles' which Eisenstein would later drop – perhaps because it sounded as if he were glorifying the methods of secret police. As Maliuta asks Ivan to let him take part in the cavalry charge of Kazan – Ivan refuses:

> Not every business is on the surface. There are other, deeper, things to heed. A candle in the wind burns brightly. A candle under the ground leads to the explosion. Stay at my side [...]. Help to exterminate rabid sedition.[75]

Fig. 47. Sixteenth-century miniature: Russian artillery besieging Kazan.

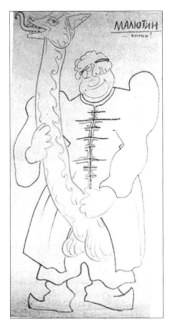

Thirdly, ancient guns, with their figurehead muzzles, made Ivan's gunmen an easy target for jokes. Take the old manuscript miniature depicting Russian artillery in action during the siege of Kazan (fig. 47 – note the ensconced Tartars drawing their bows against the cannons while Kurbsky's cavalry is waiting in the wings) and look at it through Eisenstein's eyes. The way the gunmen are shown holding their guns in this rather awkward drawing makes the latter unwittingly phallic – a *quid pro quo* that Eisenstein, with his gusto for puns on arms and sex, lays bare in his 'costume sketch for Maliuta' (fig. 48). Here was the Rabelaisian moment Eisenstein wanted his merry hangman to have.

Indeed, this picture (presented, straight-facedly, to the costume artist Lidia Naumova) is more than an eccentric aside the likes of which Eisenstein used to ladle out, galore, to the members of the crew. It is also a character study and a tribute to the legendary hero of eighteenth-century Russian obscene poetry, called Luka Mudishchev (Luke The Big-Dick) –

> About this man I will say this
> That though by fate he was not blessed
> That fate bestowed him with a penis
> The likes of which cannot be guessed[76]

– or, more exactly, to his sixteenth-century ancestor:

> That older Big-Dick called Porfeery
> Who served the court under Ivan's rule,
> To make the grim Tsar look more cheery
> Would toss up weights with his big tool.

> In keeping with Tsar Ivan's will
> One day he wielded his dick

It took one strike for him to kill
All those of whom the Tsar was sick.[77]

All this – the bawdy poem and the Rabelaisian drawing – makes up, of course, a backstage kind of knowledge, colourful, but arguably anecdotal. Is there much, one may ask, that we can do with it as regards the actual movie? The answer depends on the angle we take. There may be nothing much on the surface, but let me draw an analogy from art. Some pictures conceal a 'bonus image', an anamorphic segment (like the famous long-faced skull concealed in Holbein's *Ambassadors* at the National Gallery) that opens when we agree to part with the comfort of the frontal view – though, to make it work, you must know the angle you are required to assume. *Ivan the Terrible* is a picture like that – it yields up more at the angle of the kind of knowledge I have been trying to impart. If we attempt, for example, a 'Rabelaisian' view of the scene showing Maliuta (fig. 49) about to behead two unbending boyars (fig. 50) it will not be hard to identify in its last two shots (figs 51 and 52) two Freudian toys – phallic symbolism and the figure of castration. We should not, of course, mistake any of this for a clue – neither to the meaning of this scene nor to the character of Maliuta (no more than we should think that Holbein's skull gives the 'meaning' of his painting); rather, these shots document a range of ideas 'stuffed' into this character at different stages of making, from Caroline Spurgeon's idea of the body image buried in the verbal imagery of Shakespeare's tragedies to less extravagant ones derived from psychoanalysis. The visual pun cued by figures 51 and 52, for instance, is a fossil of Eisenstein's life-long affair with Freudian ideas, as is, among many other things, his drawing of circa 1931 (fig. 53) which depicts naked lady Macbeth (Eisenstein's favourite

Fig. 49. Execution: Maliuta prepares.

Fig. 50. Execution: the
death row.

Fig. 51. Execution: the
sight gag.

Fig. 52. Execution: Maliuta
cuts.

drawing motif) attending to her husband's erection while ecstatically watching him behead King Duncan.

To what extent such bizarre fantasies shaped *Ivan the Terrible* is the subject of the next section, but before finishing this, let me point to another legendary prototype that predefined Mikhail Zharov's superb performance as the Tsar's 'merry hangman'. To recollect: this concept was coined because Eisenstein needed Maliuta to meet two not-easy-to-reconcile conditions – to be the bad guy of history and the good guy of the film. On the plane of history, Maliuta's gusto for killings (made evident in the scene above) made Eisenstein think of another political figure that had tickled his fancy in connection with his Mexican project, Pancho Villa. Eisenstein called Villa 'the Rabelaisian monster', illustrating the monstrousness in his memoirs with reference to Villa's preferred entertainment: 'Villa ordered the prisoners to be hanged naked so that he and his soldiers could be entertained by the sight of their last physiological reaction, peculiar to hanged men.'[78] And on the plane of the film, Eisenstein's model for Maliuta was Wallace Beery in Jack Conway's *Viva Villa!* (1934) – a character whose delight in things cruel is so disarmingly childlike that we stay on Villa's side even when he orders honey spread over a prisoner who is then fed to ants:

> Maliuta must be shaped after Villa! (After Wallace Beery!!) ... Not as a Sadist, but as a demolisher [*krushitel'*].[79]

> Perhaps in the eyes of the audience *he must seem the most fervent friend – slightly too sadistic but ...*[80] [italics for English; dots in the original]

Arguably, *Viva Villa!* was also responsible for that kind of rapport between Ivan and Maliuta which Eisenstein's 1943 working note defines (possibly rephrasing Hegel's famous parable) as 'the unity of the Tsar and the slave'.[81]

Fig. 53. Eisenstein's untitled drawing from the cycle *The Murder of King Duncan* (c. 1931).

In Conway's film Villa, too, is a fervent friend, ready to part with his life for President Francisco Madero, a moralistic ruler who, for one, questions Villa's methods of handling prisoners; Villa answers, simply:

> But Mister Madero, what are we going to do with these people? I don't think you know much about war. You know about loving people. But you can't win a revolution with love, you got to have hate. You are the good side. I'm the bad side.

Maliuta proposes the same division of labour when it turns out that the Tsar's punishing hand is bound by the promise given to his former friend Philip, the advocate of the oppressed:

> There is a way out ... There is one slave [*smerd*] ... Not even a slave, just a dog ... A redheaded dog – me, Maliuta. I'll take the Tsar's sins on my shoulders. I'll give my soul for the Tsar. I'll let my own soul burn in hell, and thus keep the sanctity of the Tsar's word unbroken.

One thing which Eisenstein meant by 'the unity of the master and the slave' was that, by taking Ivan's sins on his shoulders, Maliuta also takes control over him – takes it away from Philip, who had won Ivan over in the previous scene (figs 20 and 21). If we take a closer look at the execution scene discussed a moment ago (fig. 49), we will notice a tiny detail whose inconspicuousness makes it even chillier: in the wall behind the executioner, there is a little window in which we can discern a hand – it is Ivan watching the show; when it is done, he comes out, makes a Kabuki gesture and utters a pithy ruling: *Malo!* [Not enough]. To adduce Eisenstein's words from another working note, 'Maliuta holds Ivan "by blood".'[82]

Stalin, by the way, was not enthusiastic about Eisenstein's merry hangman – neither, as it follows from the record of the Kremlin meeting, was he happy about the idea of Ivan being manipulated by anyone: 'Everyone tells him what he ought to do, he does not take decisions himself.'[83] As for Maliuta, the transcript says that 'Comrade Stalin indicated that the actor [Mikhail] Zharov had not brought sufficient gravity to his role in *Ivan the Terrible* and the result was wrong. He was not serious enough for a military commander.'[84]

Stalin's opinion was then promptly seconded by the Secretary of the Central Committee Andrei Zhdanov: 'He was not Maliuta Skuratov, more of a flibbertigibbet.'[85] It was, I am sure, the duty and function of people like Zhdanov to agree with Stalin's judgments, but in this particular case I feel there may have been something more personal. As I argued in the introductory section, everyone knew (though no one would ever dare to say) that by portraying Ivan, Eisenstein was creating the portrait of Stalin; would this imply a similar sense of identity among (and about) both rulers' henchmen? If this indeed was the case, 'wrong' must be read as 'tactless'. It was correct to show Maliuta as a killer, but it was wrong to show him no respect.

It is customary, speaking of 'Rabelaisian' moments in culture, to evoke Mikhail Bakhtin to whom we owe the idea that the 'clownish and cynical' image of human anatomy was, for Rabelais, a means to challenge 'medieval, ascetic, other-worldly ideology',[86] and, by implication, any system of values in which 'high' is synonymous with 'grave'; this then would be a good place for me to namedrop. Luck would have it that in 1974 (during my graduate years in Moscow and around a year before Bakhtin's death) the people caring for Bakhtin hired me to serve as his male nurse (Bakhtin was bed-ridden, but kept at home). Although it was understood that in this capacity I was not supposed to pose questions related to his work, from time to time I found Bakhtin quite inclined to talk. Once, he described the Soviet leadership (of that time) in terms that I find very much to the point here: '*Oni vse agilasty*', 'they are all ahilasts.' This last word, coined from the Greek *hilaros*, being Bakhtin's habitual way of referring to laughter-haters, 'anti-laughers'.

Bisexual Imagery

At the same time (to return to *Ivan* and its system of characters) Eisenstein's remark apropos 'the unity of the master and the servant' specifies that Maliuta is not really a character, but (as another of his working notes says plainly) 'the other part of Ivan'.[87] We are now back to Eisenstein's principle of *dédoublement*, which defines people around Ivan as his partial doubles – facets of his contradictory self, outer signs of Ivan's 'inner monologue',[88] which come and go, or turn into each other, depending on how Eisenstein wanted the image of Ivan to evolve.

Consider Anastasia and Fedor Basmanov. The historical Ivan was or was thought to be bisexual; rumour linked him to Fedor; people gossiped that the latter had been seen dressed in a *sarafan* (woman's dress) dancing for the Tsar. This is one end of the story. At the other end, there is Ivan's wife, Anastasia, whose early death, according to the age-old historiographic tradition, marked the end of a better period of Ivan's

Fig. 54. Ivan dancing with Basmanov. Frame enlargement from *Wings of a Serf* (1926).

reign. Consequently (and conveniently) the dynamics of this reign – from justice to tyranny – were believed to follow from the assumed change in Ivan's sexual identity. To varying degrees, works of historical fiction honour this tradition; we also find it echoed in films: figure 54, for instance, shows Leonid Leonidov – the Ivan from the silent historical melodrama *Wings of a Serf* [89] – engaged in a dance with a 1926 version of Fedor Basmanov. Eisenstein's story of Ivan, which comes in two parts, with the death of Anastasia serving as a dividing point, stays more or less within this pre-established convention.

Still, we cannot leave it at that: Eisenstein's interest in the scheme was by no means inertial or anecdotal. It is this interest that I want to discuss: firstly, what could have made Ivan's bisexuality interesting for Eisenstein and, secondly, what is interesting about the way he used it in the film. For the first part, I will look at his drawings and diary notes, then turn to the film proper. Judging by the diary, Eisenstein treated bisexuality as an interesting *philosophical* problem, and this interest is relatively easy to trace from a series of notes that appear under the heading '*b.s.*' across a longer period of time well before the making of *Ivan*. Then again, he had occasional homosexual experiences, falling into his Mexican period (around 1932), and while there is no way to tell whether or not experiences like that, or experience in general, bear on the artist's work, the whole thing did reflect on that minor genre of Eisenstein's activity, drawing and doodling, the buffer area between his private life and public image.

Here is a self-ironic drawing (fig. 55) entitled '*Yo – autoritratto*' (Spanish for 'Me – a self-portrait') which he made while waiting, in Laredo, for a US transit visa in February 1932. This is all one image (and

Fig. 55 (left). Eisenstein, '*Yo – autoritratto*' ['Me – a self-portrait'] (1932). Fig. 56 (right). Marc Chagall, *Homage to Apollinaire* (c. 1911–2).

not four drawings on one sheet of paper as it appears at first); each of its four elements depicts a different aspect of the artist's split personality. The Siamese-like figure in the centre stands for Eisenstein's 'bisexual self' (take a note of the visual joke: as one half is shown kissing the other, their lips take the shape of the equals sign: male=female). I first thought this was Eisenstein's parody of Marc Chagall's painting of 1911 (fig. 56), but Tom Gunning pointed to a likelier source for both: an emblem of androgyny found in occult books (like the one depicted in figure 57),[90] which sounds indeed very plausible, for as early as 1920, in the town of

Minsk where his army unit was stranded, Eisenstein spent some time studying arcana with the archbishop of the Rosicrucian order *Lux Astralis* (acronym: 'LA') of which Eisenstein became a young member;[91] this must also be the time when Eisenstein developed an interest in androgyny as a philosophical topic which would stay very much in his mind for the rest of his life.[92]

Fig. 57. The Androgyne as an alchemical emblem.

For instance, his diary registered who wrote what on the subject of *b.s.* In March 1940 (that is, about a year before he was approached with an offer to consider Ivan the Terrible as the possible subject of his next film), Eisenstein outlined a plan, a theoretical perspective which, at first, reads like a strange (though not so strange for Eisenstein) mix of mysticism and Marxism; the passage is a little too long to cite *in toto*, so I have made some cuts marked in square brackets, leaving Eisenstein's dots non-bracketed:

> Here is a bunch of thoughts to put in order: bisexuality as the phenomenon of regression [...]
> The idealized form of *b.s.* – Seraphita. And its swinish practice – Carlos Herrera [...]
> [Josephin] Péladan calls Christian angels androgynous [...]
> Bisexuality is ... the dynamic unity of opposites in the sphere of sex [...]
> [Bisexuality] recreates the state common to us all at the [early] stage of universal evolution. At the same time [bisexuality] belongs to the sphere of personal life. All this means that [bisexuality] is equivalent to ecstasy.
> [Péladan's androgynous] angels match Balzac's *Seraphita* (note the angelic name). And the following passage refracts the theme through the prism of Balzac's Vautrin:
> *"On aime l'androgyne, mais à moins d'être de la race de Méphistophélés, on ne le désire pas au sense possessif. Le vieux diable* [illegible] *ne voit que les reins des cohorts célestes: c'est là sa façon de sentir l'immortalité: il ravale la beauté du ciel à un frisson de Sodome. En art, ce cuistre est homosexuel et son oeil déforme la pure vision en image lascive, conception diabolique et vile par consequent ..."*
> [...]
> *B.s.* is an integral part of the *super*-human. This is why Balzac recurs to [*b.s.*] in order to depict [the *super*-human] both in its bright register – Seraphita – and in the dark one – Vautrin.
> NB: Mephistopheles as the prototype of Vautrin.[93]

This is all very general and is bound to remain so till we ask how it works for the actual film. I am not there yet (nor is Eisenstein who was unaware, at the time of writing this, that Ivan would be his next project); this note is mostly about other people's thoughts. To get to the film, what we need is a run-up which can be done in three steps:

(1) to take stock of where this or that idea comes from;
(2) to see how these ideas tallied with Eisenstein's own;
(3) to look at some shots and sketches to see what shape they take visually.

(One clarification is in order before I proceed. I know there are works in gay studies and gender studies that address the problem of bisexuality at the level of detail which makes me feel like an elephant in a china shop; nevertheless, I feel I need to tackle it, if not for its own sake, then as a tool which helped Eisenstein shape and sharpen the picture of Ivan; in other words, I am on thin ice for step one, so I had better move fast. Still, to avoid a possible confusion, I must point out that Eisenstein's notion of 'bisexuality' is broader than its sense in modern usage: as it follows from the passage above, his term *b.s.* includes both bisexual orientation and androgyny as a philosophical category.)

Consider the names. 'Seraphita' is the title character from Balzac's *Seraphita*, a novel which, to use the lofty phrase of a nineteenth-century commentator, 'was conceived ... in a moment of supreme insight and inspiration, to embody Swedenborg's noblest ideas.'[94] Central to it was the theory of divine androgyny which Emanuel Swedenborg (eighteenth-century mystic and visionary) received from Plato via alchemy: androgyny is the primordial unity of sexes to which once-divided souls are yearning to return. In the novel, the idea takes the form of an allegorical love triangle. A man named Wilfred and a young girl named Minna are both in love with a near-perfect being whom she perceives as a man called 'Seraphitus' and whom Wilfred, in his turn, calls 'Seraphita', the woman he deifies and desires; but the only true love this strange being has is for God. In the end, the SERAPH [sic] (as Balzac now calls him/her, dropping any gender ending) ascends to heaven, while Wilfred and Minna find each other's love.

Someone else mentioned in Eisenstein's diary, the French novelist and art critic Josephin Péladan, was another writer who had tailored the image of the androgyne to turn-of-the-century taste (Péladan tailored his name, too, in a manner inspired by Balzac: it is neither Joseph nor Josephine – a part added, a part of the part cropped). The androgyne of the Symbolist generation is, above all, an aesthetic creation with delicate features evoking Italian Renaissance paintings (this includes da Vinci and Botticelli, two names that became relevant to Eisenstein's future work on *Ivan*); his image is homoerotic and also forbidding: the androgyne is to be admired, but to desire him is vulgar and dangerous.

This brings us to the next pair of names in Eisenstein's collection – two fictional names from Balzac's gallery of homosexual villains featured in his *Human Comedy* cycle of novels. One is Carlos Herrera, a swinish Spanish clergyman whose 'complexion of impenetrable bronze [writes Balzac] inspired feelings of repulsion rather than attachment to the man'.[95] At one point, Herrera reveals his true identity: he is Vautrin, Balzac's proverbially demonic invert who loves evil for evil's sake; later on, this name will re-emerge more than once in Eisenstein's notes for *Ivan*. For Eisenstein, Vautrin is the shadow side of *b.s.*, the moral opposite of Seraphita.

The quotation in French (evidently, from Péladan; I am still looking) says, roughly: The androgyne exists to be loved, not coveted; only Mephistopheles, the fallen angel, looks at the heavenly creature with lustful eyes. This way Eisenstein (or Péladan) turns Mephistopheles into an old homosexual and, by the same token, accounts for the vile nature of Vautrin.

These are all murky and rather shallow waters, but things become more interesting and specific when we focus on Eisenstein's own interest in all this, which will be easier to make out if we bear in mind one thing which Eisenstein finds exciting about nearly everything – books, films, people, or their ideas: their ability to embrace contradictions, to nutshell a conflict, to cause a collision; in other words, to shape what he calls the montage-image. Look at the phrase 'Bisexuality is … the dynamic unity of opposites in the sphere of sex'. The dots in the middle are Eisenstein's, not mine: they signal his delight at the unexpected juncture between sexual philosophy and Marxist dialectics.

In what sense *b.s.* is the dynamic unity of opposites, and why, is the whole point of Eisenstein's list. Look, it says, Darwin has shown that bisexual organisms form an early stage of the evolution of species; this, in turn, explains the initial bisexuality of embryos; Freud said that bisexuality predates the development of the ego in a child; which all means (Eisenstein concludes) that bisexuality is wired deeply in the memory of everyone as a person, as a biological species, and as a member of the human race. Then again, those scientists speak of a possibility of regression, which dovetails with Eisenstein's own theory which says that the goal of art is regression to the lowest regions of generic memory. Hence this curious line: 'bisexuality equals ecstasy'. In terms of Eisenstein's poetics, the effect called ecstasy (ex-stasis, coming out of oneself) happens when art leads us beyond individual experience.

(Eisenstein had a habit of showing how things work by drawing up

diagrammatic pictures. The ideogram named 'Ecstasy' shown in figure 58 is to be read two ways: A) Progressively: Man and woman come together to engender a fetus that transcends the nutshell of the nuclear family; B) Regressively: Man and woman return to the prenatal, undifferentiated state thus transcending the dichotomy of sexes. Both readings are valid – Eisenstein was great at visual jokes.)

So far, these were but theories in diaries, but things suddenly became real and palpable in January 1941 when Andrei Zhdanov called to propose a film about Ivan: from that moment on, what had been Eisenstein's collection of other people's thoughts became the tools of his trade. Let me take a quick look at the toolkit he used to shape and shade the image of Fedor Basmanov (fig. 59), supposedly Ivan's male lover and most certainly the bloodiest figure among his infamous guards.

First, there were two literary tools named 'Vautrin' and 'Seraphita' used to distinguish what Basmanov was in Part One from what he becomes in the end. The following note (in English in the original) takes a Péladan view on Basmanov's relationship with Ivan: 'Quite possible that something happened in between. The line of *Vautrin* suppressing the line of *Seraphita*!'[96] Secondly, there were visual decisions to be made. It was not unusual for Eisenstein to build a character after pictures; to build Basmanov, Eisenstein deployed one tool named 'Botticelli' and another named 'Mikhail Vrubel':

With a black caftan on, and a dark hairpiece together with his bright eyes Kuznetsov [the actor who plays Basmanov] will look perfectly 'esoteric' (Seraphita!); [he must] look like Botticelli's Giuliano Medici![97]

Two or three words about Giuliano (fig. 60) and why Eisenstein found Botticelli's image 'esoteric'. In the 1470s Giuliano Medici was stabbed to death (in a church, while praying) by a member of a hostile clan; Botticelli made several portraits of him, all posthumous; the open window seen behind alludes to his passage to the afterlife; some art historians suggest that these portraits were painted from Giuliano's death mask, which would explain the half-closed eyes that give this face its inscrutable look; this particular picture is the one Eisenstein could have seen at the National Gallery in Washington; in the original, the clothing Giuliano is wearing is dark red, not black; but it does look black on black-and-white reproductions.

Now, back to Basmanov; his other painterly prototype is *Demon Defeated* (1901–2) (fig. 61) by the Symbolist artist Mikhail Vrubel mentioned in the following note:

> Fedor Basmanov looks a little like a very young 'demon' (after 'Demon'). By the way, [in his accusatory epistle to Ivan the historical] Kurbsky mentions a massacre of the town of Riazan by the Tsar's guards led by 'their *demonic* war lord [*demonsky voevoda*] Fedor Basmanov, his lover' (that is, the Tsar's).[98]

Fig. 61. Mikhail Vrubel, Study for *Demon Defeated* (1901–2).

Fig. 60 (top). Alessandro Botticelli. *Portrait of Giuliano de' Medici* (c.1476-1477).

Never mind Kurbsky and his piece of historical evidence (or political libel): Vrubel's 'Demon' is more instrumental. In one of Eisenstein's sketches (fig. 62), visibly Vrubelesque in manner, Basmanov has Vrubel eyes and the upper sleeves of his caftan are shaped to suggest a pair of wings. If Part Three had been made, we would have witnessed Fedor Basmanov (killed on Ivan's order) die much in the manner sad and evil spirits do in Romantic poetry and in Symbolist painting; the scenario reads:

> He is dead …
> Fedor lies on the floor,
> A fallen angel in his black robe which unfolds like wings upon the flagstones.[99]

Thirdly, there is a tool named 'Freud', or 'Freud-improved-upon', the Freud customised for Eisenstein's needs. As I said earlier on, Eisenstein conceived *Ivan the Terrible* as a monodrama which means that characters around Ivan are kinds of proxies, or avatars, which behave, mutate, exchange functions according to what is going on in the main hero's mind (his 'inner monologue', to hark back to Eisenstein's term). This concept entitled Eisenstein to treat characters with a kind of freedom no other film-maker would need or fancy. Basmanov, for instance, is only one half of a character, the other half being Ivan's wife Anastasia because the goal Eisenstein had in mind was to create a character that was androgynous in more than a figurative sense.

I know this sounds weird, but such was his plan, and it is worth looking at, since it explains a few important things about the film. Remember the old story: things go wrong when Anastasia dies and with her goes her moral influence upon Ivan. But, being a character in a monodrama – the-story-perceived-as-through-Ivan's-eye – she does not die but slips into a different character of the opposite gender. Here is a note Eisenstein made on 23 May 1942 – roughly in the middle of thinking the plan up:

Fig. 62. Eisenstein's study for Fedor Basmanov.

Fedor is *Ersatz* Anastasia.
Not only on the level of 'history' and 'life' [*fakticheski*].
He takes her place morally.
On the level of vulgar travesty [*grubo-ernicheski*] this motif already exists: the mask and the [women's] dress [*sarafan*] call to mind Anastasia! The same on a loftier note: Anastasia's eyes are closed; instead, [we see] Fedor's eyes shining in the dark.[100]

Let me plot a path through this rather sketchy note, starting from the bottom and working up. 'The same on a loftier note' alludes to the moment in Part One when Basmanov takes over; to justify it, Eisenstein stages what Freudians call *Übertragung*, or 'transference' – the term coined to explain why we fall in love not with the ones we love, but with someone to hand. Ivan is shown mourning over Anastasia in her coffin; Basmanov is standing by. Ivan looks (fig. 63) at her (fig. 64), then turns his

Fig. 63. Ivan looks at the face in the bier.

Fig. 64. The dead Anastasia.

Fig. 65. Ivan looks at
Fedor Basmanov.

Fig. 66. Basmanov looks
at Ivan: note the light
falling from above.

Fig. 67. Basmanov
implicates Yefrosinya: note
the light falling from below.

head (fig. 65) to look at Basmanov whose face is lit and framed to look beautifully seraphic (fig. 66). Later in the film, this face occasionally undergoes a Jekyll-to-Hyde transformation: for instance, figure 67 shows Basmanov planting a suspicion in Ivan's mind. However, the full complexity of Eisenstein's bisexual design only becomes apparent towards the end of the film, in the scene which the note (two lines up) defines as 'vulgar travesty'.

The reference is, of course, to the all-male revel in the course of which Basmanov, who wears a folksy women's dress (known as a 'sarafan') and female mask, is shown singing and dancing amid the male corps de ballet (fig. 68). This travesty, the note says, must call to mind Anastasia – but not because the mask looks like her – it does not, nor are

Fig. 68. Basmanov's
dance with the mask.

there any other signs of obvious likeness. Rather, Eisenstein counted on our *structural* memory – in this case, on our ability to correlate symmetrical patterns across large spaces of time. Remember, the film opens with the crowning of Ivan, and ends with the mock crowning of Vladimir, a chilly ceremony since soon afterwards he is killed; by the same token, the event that takes place before the mock crowning, Basmanov dancing and all, echoes, darkly, the wedding of Ivan and Anastasia – the second large scene of the film after the crowning of Ivan.

This symmetry is not one of patterning and situations only, but also one of details. During the wedding, the guests are treated to white swans carried in by a train of servants (fig. 69). The same bird, much in the same manner, is offered to poor Vladimir at what will turn out to be his last meal – only these swans are black (fig. 70). Swans come (needless to say) from the antiquated inventory of Symbolist art – antiquated, of

Fig. 69. Wedding feast,
Part One: the white swans.

Fig. 70. All-male banquet,
Part Two: the black swans.

Fig. 71. Swan's black head
in the dark: Vladimir gasps
(Part Two).

Fig. 72. Part One:
Anastasia smiles at the
wedding swans.

course, relative to 1945; turn-of-the-century iconographic tradition links
them to chastity and death.[101] We could, if we wished, go on from there
and explore what Eisenstein makes of it, for instance when we see
Vladimir slightly scared at the sight of what Germans call *Trauerschwan*
– the black swan of grief (figs 70 and 71), or when he adds to the white
swan train the soundtrack with the nuptial chant in which the bride is
called *lebed belaya*, 'white swan', and how this motif colours our
perception of Anastasia's radiant face (fig. 72). But this sort of a
discussion would be a discussion of meaning which is precisely what I
would like to stop short of.

Before I go on, let me pause to look back – not to summarise, but
rather to apologise for what I have been doing. First, there was nothing
methodical or mechanical about the making of *Ivan* as I am afraid my
crude account at times makes it sound. It was not as if Eisenstein came
with all that luggage of thoughts about sexuality to unload upon *Ivan*; on
the contrary, he perceived the ideas as looming large in the material itself.
But, after all, my goal has not been to describe what was going on in
Eisenstein's mind, but to take stock of his film-making equipment.
Secondly, it is hard to speak about symbolism of any sort and not to
conjure the ghost of interpretation. Symbols are mostly vapid as far as
what they mean and interestingly different as to their usage. What I was
trying to do was not to explain the meaning of *Ivan* but to explain *Ivan* as
a picture.

Eisenstein's 'Ivan' and Eisenstein's Freud

Let me explain what I just said. 'To explain *Ivan* as a picture' is not about
what this or that element in it is meant to evoke; it is about why this or that

element is the way it is. In the first case ('textual reading') meaning is the ultimate goal; in the second, meaning is a means to an end ('contextual reading'). Psychoanalysis (understood here, needless to say, not as a trend in film studies but as part of Eisenstein's intellectual environment) is a case in point. Eisenstein's writings abound in references to Freud and Rank, and to lesser figures in the field (some of whom Eisenstein knew personally) but, easy as this makes it for us to connect his films to psychologists' ideas, easily is hardly the way of doing it. We risk trivialising *Ivan* if we tap Eisenstein's Freud with an eye to see 'what means what' in Eisenstein's film; 'what is Freud doing here' sounds like a better question. In the world we are looking at, ideas have no intrinsic value: they go for the price of their visual corollary.

Take a study drawn in March 1942 (fig. 73). On the same sheet of paper we find depicted two scenes that, in the film, are some ten minutes apart and, if we stick to the story, have little to do with each other. Written above both drawings, however, is Eisenstein's remark 'Full analogy as to positioning and acting' – an analogy which, according to the phrase in angled brackets below the drawings, explains 'why Vladimir blabbed it out'. Another remark (upper right) specifies the business common to both scenes: 'Byplay with Vladimir's hair'.

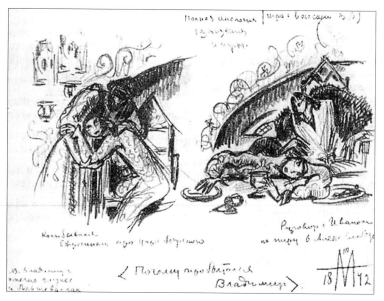

74 Fig. 73. This study juxtaposes two scenes from Part Two: Vladimir with his mother; Vladimir at Ivan's banquet.

Fig. 74. Vladimir at Ivan's banquet.

Fig. 75. Vladimir with his mother.

Let us first identify the scenes in question. The drawing on the right refers to a scene that takes place during the feast in the banqueting room; it depicts Ivan and his tipsy cousin Vladimir as the latter 'blabs out' the fact that the boyars conspire to kill the Tsar (fig. 74). The left-hand drawing shows an earlier scene in which Vladimir is shown in his mother's room, dozing off on her lap: Yefrosinya caresses his hair and sings him a lullaby song (fig. 75). (Keep in mind that the lullaby scene follows the scene in which Yefrosinya and the disloyal clergyman Pimen conspire to dispatch Ivan and replace him with Vladimir.)

The two scenes, indeed, use similar staging-cum-acting schemata: in both, we see Vladimir reclining, while the other character is seen towering behind him; in each, the hand of the sitting character touches Vladimir's head. Why? Two more pieces of evidence found among Eisenstein's working notes make Freud responsible both for the way these figures are positioned and for the fact that their positions are similar in both shots. Why is Ivan sitting behind the reclining Vladimir? A preparatory note for the feast scene comments, in German: '*Situation der Patientencouch*'[102] – an allusion to Freud's consulting room in Vienna, which was furnished so that the patient, lying back on a couch, did not face the therapist, only hearing his voice. Staging the shot with Freud in mind (Eisenstein thought) provided one answer to 'why Vladimir blabs it out': sitting behind Vladimir helps Ivan (a detective by purpose, a therapist by method) to lift the control of Vladimir's superego.

Then, there is another why to be answered: why did Ivan's scheme prove effective? To puzzle it out, we need to do the following. First, add to the study we've just discussed two more pieces of evidence: the drawing to the left of it seen in figure 73 (which is a study for the lullaby scene seen in figure 75) and Eisenstein's note that explains the connection between the two. Second, in order to understand Eisenstein's comment, go back to Freud's consulting room and look up a side-effect Freud has observed some couch treatments may lead to, namely, that in the process of the treatment, the patient tends to shift on to the therapist some of their earlier emotional attachments (in psychoanalytic literature the effect is known as a form of 'transference', or *Übertragung*; we have seen Eisenstein, at the end of Part One, making use of a different form of it). Once all the four pieces are in place, the picture of Eisenstein's intentions looks as follows: Ivan's questioning of Vladimir proves effective (thinks Eisenstein as he sketches Vladimir dozing off, his head on his mother's lap, for an earlier scene) because the latter transfers onto Ivan the experienced of being mothered:

> The situation of the 'Lullaby' [scene] is *absolutely* analogous to the scene with Ivan.
> Yefrosinya uses the *same* gesture to caress Vladimir's hair.
> Even the kiss!!!
> And then it becomes absolutely natural that [during the feast at Ivan's] as soon as Vladimir finds himself in the *same* childhood situation he blabs out in a *childlike manner* the things that he had heard in a similar situation. (*Great!*).
> NB: good here: Vlad[imir] finds himself in a childhood situation which lifts the inhibiting factor. And then, those [hand] passes that help to undo inhibitions![103]

Let us assume we have answered the whys about Eisenstein's design; some will feel it is psychologically credible, others – those who doubt the human psyche works in Freudian ways – may still appreciate the boldness of Eisenstein's visual idea or his trust in Freud. But even then many will be sceptical as to how Eisenstein was going to communicate this parallelism to the viewer. Indeed, the whole plan is likely to meet with two common-sense objections: one, how on earth could one hope for these things to be noticed and memorised; and the other: even then, who on earth would be able to understand what this means? In other words: what viewer, aside from some lightning analyst endowed with total recall, would find meaning in a few ephemeral similarities between two non-contiguous shots? Let me take on the second objection leaving the first – the question of recall – for the next (and the last) section. Against everything the above example may seem to suggest, I insist that the key question of psychoanalysis, 'what's the meaning of this', becomes vacuous at the level of art. Eisenstein's films make sense not by virtue of what they tell, but owing to what they *do* to the viewer. Hermeneutics, with all its equipment and cognitive premises, was alien to Eisenstein who preferred the approach he dubbed 'operational': 'I call my "system of aesthetics," which I must eventually assemble, an "operational aesthetics". How to do it.'[104]

The Return to the Womb

To put it in our terms, operational film theory treats the stream of data between the film and the viewer not as one of messages, but as one of instructions: the film is a set of orders issued not to analyse, but to obey. According to Eisenstein, the way we react to films is by re-acting, 're-enacting' the seen. Re-enacting in what sense? Somatically, for instance: say, I see Vladimir's body take that 'childhood position': subliminally, my own body perceives this as a signal to follow suit. True empathy, according to Eisenstein, is born in the muscles, not in the brain.

This last point, about somatic empathy, is not in itself that uncommon, and may even appear naïve, insofar as it draws, uncritically, on broad theories of empathy current in eighteenth- and nineteenth-century aesthetics. What *was* uncommon (and instrumental for *Ivan*) was that Eisenstein found a way to connect somatic empathy and the 'trauma of birth', the concept borrowed from the psychologist Otto Rank, Freud's brilliant (though ultimately unwelcome) disciple. According to Rank, the master key to human culture was our prenatal experience – the emotional memory of being born which Rank believed

Fig. 76. The flashback: Ivan as a boy witnesses his mother being murdered. Note the beam of light.

stayed dormant in one's mind and body throughout one's life. The task of the artist (according to Eisenstein) is to bring out this memory; the way it could be done was to reproduce prenatal experience in the medium of film.

To see Rank work in *Ivan*, take another pair of identically shaped shots – one from the ending, another from the 'prologue' to the film.[105] The latter, showing Ivan as a child witness his mother being murdered, re-enacts, with due alterations, Rank's study of 'infantile anxiety' (fig. 76). Alone in the dark church, young Ivan is on the beam of light coming from the door through which his mother has just disappeared. Compare this scene to this passage from Rank's book *The Trauma of Birth*:

> [L]et us investigate the typical case of infantile anxiety which occurs when the child is left alone *in a dark room* (usually the bedroom at bed-time). This situation reminds the child, who still is close to the experience of the primal trauma, of the womb situation – with the important difference that the child is now consciously separated from the mother whose womb is only 'symbolically' replaced by the dark room or warm bed.[106]

The visual pattern that evokes Rank's 'womb situation' – darkness pierced by a slit of light – re-emerges at the end of the film when we see Vladimir (the unfortunate blabber) walking towards inexorable death (fig. 77). The birth trauma connection is a little less obvious here, but the point is that Rank (and Eisenstein) believed that the way minds (and cultures) cope with the problem of mortality is to imagine death as a

Fig. 77. The finale:
Vladimir enters the
cathedral to be murdered
there. Note the beam.

return to the mother's womb; hence, such symbols as Mother Earth, the lap of the Church, or the very custom of putting the dead in a casket and burying them under the ground. The mind of the death-bound (here, Vladimir's) plays back the trauma of birth; note that in the childhood scene the boy Ivan looks *up* the beam of light while Vladimir, after a slight hesitation as he steps on it, turns and walks in the opposite direction, towards darkness.

To conclude, let me mention what I think was a special appeal Rank's writings held for Eisenstein – one thing that made them a more useful tool than Freud's. Most of Freud's material is verbal, whereas when Rank speaks of prenatal experiences the very nature of the concept impels him to operate with primary sensory material – such as light and darkness, the sense of movement, gravity, temperature, indistinct sounds – much of which is cinema's material as well. There was also another thing about Rank that helped his theory coalesce with Eisenstein's film practice. The main problem other psychologists (including Freud) had with the idea of prenatal memory was that such faculties as sight and hearing develop some time after birth – how can the infant then experience birth as a tumultuous affair of 'coming out to light?'[107] This would posit that prenatal memory – provided there was such a thing – was stored in some kind of undifferentiated sensorium, in the body itself, as it were.

Discouraging as it may appear to the scientist, this vague hypothesis gave Eisenstein an idea to stage a surprising experiment. As poor Vladimir goes like a lamb to the slaughter, Eisenstein told the cinematographer Andrei Moskvin to light the interior of the church in such a way that it suggests the space inside the mother's womb; legendary for his imperturbable face, Moskvin is said to have nodded and made the necessary arrangements (fig. 78). Eisenstein also asked the sound operator Boris Volsky to record the background singing in such a manner that it rings like birth pangs[108] – for he believed in somatic empathy, that is, in the capacity of our bodies to resonate in response to convulsive ('prenatal') sound.

I am not writing this in order to pass a judgment on whether or not the experiment succeeded (though I do encourage the inquisitive reader to replay the sequence in question, found in Chapter 19 on your DVD version of Part Two, and check whether Volsky's intentionally fitful recording rings a bell). For me, it succeeds on the strength of being there, for (to generalise the point) the pliancy of our cognitive apparatus is such that the awareness of Eisenstein's intentions makes us accessories to his design.

Fig. 78. The womb of the Cathedral.

Fig. 79. The last unction: the shot I think I remember from 1958.

Feedback exists between awareness and perception, or reading Eisenstein (and this book) would be a waste of time. When, after more than a decade of shelf-life, *Ivan* Part Two finally saw the screen I was eight, vacationing with my grandmother (Anna Grishina) in Gudauti (then Soviet Georgia). She took me to the film (both parts were shown without a break) and whether or not it was the first film I ever saw, it is the first I remember having seen, though, of course, there is little I can tell about the film from that first viewing. The few things I can glean are: flying glances; the sense of something bad happening (to me or to people in the film), the meaning of which escaped me. Visually, the dark spaces I remember as frightening; I also recall a feeling of pressure and suffocation. The only film image I can pin down is from the Last Unction scene, the moment when the silver-bound bible covers Ivan's face (fig. 79). I do not have much to add in terms of detail, but if such a thing as 'infantile anxiety' exists I must have been close to experiencing it, and what caused it had more to do with sensory impact than with anything else. Now that I have read some of Rank and Eisenstein on Rank, it all seems to make sense. I do not care if this sense has been supplied to me by the wisdom of hindsight – as long as the back-and-forth between knowledge and feeling sharpens our perception of the film.

IVAN THE TERRIBLE

NOTES

. . . .

1 Naum Kleiman, '*Formula finala*' [The Formula of the Ending], *Kinovedcheskije Zapiski* [Film Scholarship Annals], no. 38, 1998, pp. 100–32.

2 Leonid Kozlov, 'The Artist and the Shadow of Ivan', in Richard Taylor and Derek Spring (eds), *Stalinism and Soviet Cinema* (London: Routledge, 1993), pp. 109–30.

3 Kristin Thompson, *Eisenstein's Ivan the Terrible: A Neoformalist Analysis* (Princeton, NJ: Princeton University Press, 1981).

4 *DVD Eisenstein: The Sound Years* (New York: Criterion, 2001): disks 2–3.

5 *Kultura i zhizn* [Culture and Life], September 4, 1946.

6 'Stalin, Molotov and Zhdanov on *Ivan the Terrible, Part Two* (1947)', trans. by Richard Taylor and William Powell, in Richard Taylor (ed.), *The Eisenstein Reader* (London: BFI Publishing, 1998), p. 160.

7 Ibid., p. 161.

8 Ibid., p. 162.

9 Ibid.

10 Ibid.

11 RGALI [Russian State Archive for Literature and Art], *fond* 1923, *opis'* 2, *edinitsa khranenija* 1176, list 53. Herewith, all references to Eisenstein's collection of papers catalogued under the number 1923 in this archive will appear in short, e.g. the above as RGALI 2/1176/53 (the last number is omitted whenever the item consists of a single sheet. All (double-)underlined segments in quotations from Eisenstein's writings are his own; italics are used to mark English or any other non-Russian words in the original.

12 Wassily Kandinsky and Franz Marc (eds), *The Blaue Reiter Almanac*, trans. by Henning Falkenstein (New York: The Viking Press, 1974), p. 95. Eisenstein quotes Schoenberg's essay in German.

13 RGALI 2/1164/18.

14 K. Valishevskii, *Ivan Groznyi* (Moscow: Obschestvennaia pol'za, 1912), p. 134.

15 RGALI 1/554/44; on the conceptual importance of this etymology see Leonid Kozlov, '*Ten Groznogo i khudozhnik*' [The Shadow of Grozny and the Artist], *Kinovedcheskie Zapiski* [Film Studies Annals] no. 15, 1992, p. 44.

16 RGALI 1/568/1.

17 RGALI 1/586/11.

18 This song originally belonged elsewhere. It had been recorded for a discarded scene in which the *Oprichniki* – Tsar's guards – would have been shown taking an oath to protect Ivan from conspiracies.

19 RGALI 1/568/35; see also 1/568/83.

20 RGALI 2/1172/36. Here and elsewhere round and angled brackets are Eisenstein's. Square brackets are mine.

21 Eisenstein calls Piranesi's structures 'telescopic' (Sergei Eisenstein, *Izbrannye proizvedenija v shesti tomakh* [Selected Works in Six Volumes] (Moscow: *Iskusstvo*, 1964, vol. 3, p. 180; henceforth as IP 1…6) – he used this metaphor (as that of 'triple arbalest') to refer to the story structure as well (IP 3, pp. 185–7.)

22 RGALI 2/1180.

23 Ibid.

24 Ibid.

25 Pierre Bourdieu, *The Logic of Practice*, trans. by Richard Nice (Stanford: Stanford University Press, 1990), pp. 165, 228.

26 I am indebted to Richard Wortman for the historical details on the ritual of Russian coronation. One may also cautiously suggest that Eisenstein borrowed this move from Napoleon who is said to have whisked the crown from the Pope's hands at the time of his coronation.

27 Alexander Nechvolodov, *Skazaniia o russkoi zemle* [Tales of the Russian Land] (St. Petersburg: Gos. tip., 1913), vol. 4.

28 *Ivan the Terrible. A Screenplay by Sergei M. Eisenstein*, trans. by Ivor Montagu and Herbert Marshall (New York: Simon and Schuster, 1962), pp. 117–18. It is not clear why and at what stage Eisenstein discarded this scene; we know that he thought about casting it – his friend theatre critic Iosif Yuzovsky was to play the chief jester. (*Kinovedcheskie zapiski* [Film Studies Annals], no. 38, p. 63).

29 Alan H. Nelson, 'Mechanical Wheels of Fortune, 110–1547', *Journal of Warburg and Courtauld Institutes*, vol. 43 no. 43, 1980, pp. 227–33; Barbara Ann Day, 'Representing Aging and Death in French Culture', *French Historical Studies*, vol. 17 no. 3, Spring 1992, pp. 688–724.

30 Boethius, *The Consolation of Philosophy*, trans. by W. V. Cooper (London: J. M. Dent & Sons, 1902), pp. 28–8.

31 RGALI 1/570/10. Although, in a technical sense, at this stage of pre-production, *Ivan* was still envisaged as a two-episode picture, conceptually it was a trilogy in two parts.

32 RGALI 1/570/11.

33 Ibid.

34 Kleiman, '*Formula finala*' [The Formula of the Ending], p. 107. The drawing Kleiman is referring to is reproduced in Jay Leida and Zina Voinov, *Eisenstein at Work* (New York: Pantheon House, 1982), p. 145.

35 Reproduced in Nechvolodov, *Skazaniia*.

36 IP 6, p. 496.

37 If there is one, the source for this fresco is not clear. As Kristin Thompson convincingly shows, Eisenstein's figure finds no direct parallels in Orthodox iconography. See Thompson, *Eisenstein's Ivan the Terrible*, p. 189.

38 IP 6, p. 305.

39 RGALI 1/576/26.

40 RGALI 2/1721/10.

41 RGALI 1/565/18.

42 RGALI 2/1166/29.

43 RGALI 1/585; quoted after: Mira Meilakh, *Izobrazitelnaya stilistika pozdnikh filmov Eizensteina* [Visual Style in Eisenstein's Late Films] (Leningrad: Iskusstvo, 1971), p. 103.

44 B. V. Mikhailovsky and B. I. Purishev, *Ocherki istorii drevnerusskoi monumentalnoi zhivopisi* [Essays on the History of Russian Monumental Painting] (Moscow, Leningrad: Iskusstvo, 1941, pp. 65, 217). My thanks go to Simone Tai for locating this source.

45 Thompson, *Eisenstein's Ivan the Terrible*, p. 191.

46 RGALI 2/1165/30.

47 IP 3, p. 320.

48 I am indebted to Valentina Freimane for this term.

49 Serge Strenkovsky, *The Art of Make-up*, ed. by Elizabeth S. Taber (New York: Dutton, 1937), plate 13.

50 Sergei Eisenstein, *Memuary* [Memoirs] (Moscow: Trud; Muzei Kino, 1997), vol. 2, p. 60. The English translation of this book appeared as Richard Taylor (ed.), *Beyond the Stars: The Memoirs of Sergei Eisenstein*, trans. by William Powell (London: BFI Publishing; Calcutta: Seagull Books, 1995).

51 I am indebted to Sid Gottlieb for sending me Orson Welles' 23 May 1945 column that appeared in the *New York Post*. James Naremore discusses Welles' view of Eisenstein's film in the chapter 'The Radicalization of Style', in *The Magic World of Orson Welles* (New York: Oxford University Press, 1978).

52 RGALI 2/1176/53.

53 Ibid.

54 Ibid.

55 RGALI 2/1176/54.

56 Ibid. A scene similar to the one described by Eisenstein exists in one of Fred Astaire's musicals of the 1930s.

57 RGALI 2/1176/54.

58 Welles, *The Magic World*.

59 Caroline Spurgeon, *Shakespeare's Imagery and What It Tells Us* (Cambridge: Cambridge University Press, 1935), p. 347; Eisenstein quotes this book amply in his 1937 book *Montage* fully published only two years ago, *Montazh 1937*, ed., commented and introduced by Naum Kleiman (Moscow: Film Museum, 2000). An incomplete but useful version of this book appeared in English, in Michael Glenny and Richard Taylor (eds), *S. M. Eisenstein, Selected Works*, vol. 2: *Towards a Theory of Montage* (London: BFI Publishing, 1991).

60 *The Tragedy of Coriolanus*, in *The Riverside Shakespeare* (Boston: Houghton Mifflin Company, 1974), p. 1397.

61 Alfred Winterstein, *Der Ursprung der Tragödie: ein psychoanalytischer Beitrag zur Geschichte des griechischen Theaters* (Vienna: Internationaler Psychoanalytischer Verlag, 1925).

62 See *Montazh 1937*, pp. 221–9.

63 RGALI 2/1177/16; see also 2/1176/31.

64 *Montazh 1937*, pp. 246–7.

65 RGALI 2/128/31; quoted after Manana Andronikova, *Ot prototipa k obrazu* [From Prototype to Image] (Moscow: Nauka, 1974), p. 78.

66 Ibid.

67 RGALI 1/577/7.

68 RGALI 1/583/47.

69 RGALI 2/1173/24.

70 RGALI 1/570/39.

71 RGALI 1/570/40.

72 RGALI 1/570/45.

73 James Agee, ['Ivan the Terrible'], *The Nation*, 26 April 1947, p. 495.

74 RGALI 1/553/92.

75 RGALI 1/539/24. In this early version the parable is addressed to Grigorii Basmanov – later he will be replaced by Maliuta.

76 Anonymous [ascribed to Ivan Barkov], 'Luke The Big-Dick', in V. Butkov and V. Dubov (eds), *Shalosti geniev: erotika i nepristoinosti v russkoi poeʒii* [Pranking Geniuses: Erotica and Obscenities in Russian Poetry] (Riga: Avize, 1992), p. 120; the responsibility for this awkward but enthusiastic translation I share with my USC student Chris Gilman.

77 Ibid., pp. 120–1.

78 Eisenstein, *Beyond the Stars*, p. 420.

79 RGALI 1/553/52.

80 RGALI 1/553/55.

81 RGALI 2/128/31; quoted after Andronikova, *Ot prototipa k obraʒu* [From Prototype to Image], p. 78.

82 IP 6, p. 495.

83 'Stalin, Molotov and Zhdanov on *Ivan the Terrible, Part Two* (1947)', p. 160.

84 Ibid., p. 166.

85 Ibid.

86 Mikhail Bakhtin, *The Dialogic Imagination*, ed. by Michael Holquist (Austin: University of Texas Press, 1996), p. 171.

87 Ibid.

88 RGALI 2/128/31; quoted after Andronikova, *Ot prototipa k obraʒu* [From Prototype to Image], p. 78

89 Directed by Yuri Tarich, written by Viktor Shklovsky.

90 Alexander Roob, *Alchemy & Mysticism* (New York: Taschen, 1997), pp. 450–64.

91 On Eisenstein the Rosicrucian see his book of memoirs, *Beyond the Stars* (pp. 78–83) and the biographical study on Boris Zubakin, the master of the order: A. I. Nemirovsky, B. I. Ukolova, *Svet ʒveʒd ili poslednij russkij rozenkreitser* [Light of Stars, or the Last Russian Rosicrucian] (Moscow: Progress–Kultura, 1994), pp. 19, 95.

92 Shearer West, *Fin de Siècle* (New York: Overlook Press, 1993), p. 81.

93 RGALI 1/1536/19–20.

94 George Frederic Parson's 'Introduction' to Honoré de Balzac, *Seraphita* (Boston: Roberts Brothers, 1889), p. xxv.

95 Honoré de Balzac, *Lost Illusions. The Complete Works of Honoré de Balzac*, vol. 8 (Boston, New York: Jefferson Press, 1901), p. 323.

96 Ibid.

97 IP 6, p. 513.

98 RGALI 1/520/39.

99 Sergei Eisenstein, *Ivan the Terrible* (London, Boston: Faber and Faber, 1989), p. 253.

100 IP 6, p. 512.

101 See the excellent essay by Reinhold Heller, 'Edvard Munch's Vision and the Symbolist Swan', *Art Quarterly*, vol. 36 no. 3, 1973, pp. 209–49.

102 RGALI 1/557/62.

103 Ibid.

104 Eisenstein, *Beyond the Stars*, p. 500.

105 Originally, the childhood scene I am going to discuss was not a flashback but a prologue which was supposed to open the film. At the last moment Eisenstein was forced by censors to shift the prologue to Part Two.

106 Otto Rank, *The Trauma of Birth* (New York: Dover Publications, 1993), pp. 11–12.

107 Sigmund Freud, 'Inhibitions, Symptoms and Anxiety', in *The Standard Edition of the Complete Psychological Works of Sigmund Freud*, trans. under the general editorship of James Strachey, in collaboration with Anna Freud, assisted by Alix Strachey and Alan Tyson (London: Hogarth Press and the Institute of Psycho-analysis, 1953–74), vol. 20, pp. 135–6. I am indebted to Harry Trosman for pointing to this source.

108 This, as well as the previously mentioned production anecdote, has come down to us as written down by Naum Kleiman during his conversations with Volsky and Moskvin.

CREDITS

Ivan the Terrible

Soviet Union
1945
Director
Sergei Eisenstein
Scenario/Dialogue
Sergei Eisenstein
Cinematography
Interior Scenes:
Andrei Moskvin
Exterior Scenes:
Eduard Tisse
Designer
Iosif Shpinel, based on
sketches by Sergei Eisenstein
Music
Sergei Prokofiev

Production Companies
Mosfilm (Moscow)/TsOKS
(Alma Ata)
Administrators
A. Eidus, I. Soluyanov,
I. Vakar
Associate Directors
Lev Indenbom, Boris
Sveshnikov
Assistant Directors
Valentina Kuznetsova, I. Bir,
B. Buneev, F. Soluyanov
Cameraman
Viktor Dombrovsky
Editing Assistant
Esfir Tobak
Set Decorator
Nadezhda Buzina
Costumes
Lidia Naumova,
M. Safonova, based on
sketches by Sergei Eisenstein
Make-up
Vasilii Goriunov
Music Conductor
Abram Stasevich
Lyrics
Vladimir Lugovskoy, based
on folk songs and texts by
Sergei Eisenstein

Choreography
R. Zakharov
Sound
Vladimir Bogdankevich,
Boris Volsky

Cast
Nikolai Cherkasov
Tsar Ivan IV
Lyudmila Tselikovskaya
Tsarina Anastasia
Romanovna
Serafima Birman
Boyarina Yefrosinya
Staritskaya, Ivan's aunt
Mikhail Nazvanov
Prince Andrei Kurbsky
Mikhail Zharov
Tsar's guard Maliuta
Skuratov
Amvrosii Buchma
Tsar's guard Aleksei
Basmanov
Mikhail Kuznetsov
his son, Tsar's guard Fedor
Basmanov
Pavel Kadochnikov
Vladimir Andreyevich
Staritsky, Tsar's cousin
Andrei Abrikosov
Fedor Kolychev, later Philip,
Metropolitan Bishop of
Moscow
Aleksandr Mgebrov
Novgorod's Archbishop
Pimen
Maksim Mikhailov
Archdeacon
Vsevolod Pudovkin
Nikola, a prophet-beggar
Valentina Kuznetsova
a smiling woman in the
church
Aleksandr Rumnev
the foreigner
Semyon Timoshenko
Kaspar von Oldenbock,
Livonian ambassador

Vladimir Balashov
Pyotr Volynets, the assassin
Erik Pyryev
Ivan IV as a boy
Ada Voitsik
Elena Glinskaya, Ivan's
mother
Pavel Massalsky
King Sigismund of Poland

Part One
Premiere 30 December 1944;
release 16 January 1945
9,006 feet
2,745 metres
12 reels
99 minutes
Awards: 1946 Stalin Prize,
first grade; 1946 Locarno
Film Festival, best
cinematography.

Part Two (Boyars' Plot)
Banned in 1946, Premiere 1
September 1958
7,785 feet
2,373 metres
11 reels
85 minutes

Credits checked by
Markku Salmi,
BFI Filmographic Unit

BIBLIOGRAPHY AND SOURCES

· ·

SOURCE MATERIALS

Eisenstein: The Sound Years [includes a DVD version of the film with outtakes, tests and scholarly commentaries by Joan Neuberger and Yuri Tsivian] (New York: Criterion, 2001), disks 2–3.

Eisenstein, Sergei, *Ivan the Terrible* [includes the film transcript and Eisenstein's scenario for Part Three] (London, Boston: Faber and Faber, 1989).

——, *Ivan the Terrible. A Screenplay by Sergei M. Eisenstein*, trans. by Ivor Montagu and Herbert Marshall (New York: Simon and Schuster, 1962).

——, *Drawings* (Moscow: Iskusstvo, 1961).

[Kleiman, Naum] *Neizvestnyi "Ivan Grozny"* [The Unknown *Ivan the Terrible*; a CD ROM; includes preparatory and discarded material with a voice-over commentary by Naum Kleiman] (Moscow: Gosfilmofond / Muzei Kino, 1998).

'Stalin, Molotov and Zhdanov on *Ivan the Terrible, Part Two* (1947)', trans. by Richard Taylor and William Powell, in Richard Taylor (ed.), *The Eisenstein Reader*, (London: BFI Publishing, 1998).

EISENSTEIN ON *IVAN*

'The People of One Film' [on the shooting crew of *Ivan*], in Richard Taylor (ed.), *S. M. Eisenstein, Selected Works*, vol. 3: *Writings 1934–47* (London: BFI Publishing, 1996), pp. 305–16.

'From Lectures on Music and Colour in *Ivan the Terrible*', in Taylor (ed.), *Selected Works*, vol. 3, pp. 317–38.

Beyond the Stars: The Memoirs of Sergei Eisenstein, ed. by Richard Taylor, trans. by William Powell (London: BFI Publishing; Calcutta: Seagull Books, 1995).

BOOKS ON *IVAN* (CHRONOLOGICAL LISTING)

Roberge, Gaston, *Eisenstein's 'Ivan the Terrible': An Analysis* (Calcutta: Chitrabani, 1980).

Thompson, Kristin, *Eisenstein's Ivan the Terrible: A Neoformalist Analysis* (Princeton, NJ: Princeton University Press, 1981).

Kinovedcheskije zapiski [Film Scholarship Annals], no. 38, 1998, special issue on *Ivan Groznyi*.

SOME BOOKS THAT CONTAIN SIGNIFICANT SECTIONS ON *IVAN*

Andronikova, Manana, *Ot prototipa k obrazu* [From Prototype to Image] (Moscow: Nauka, 1974).

Aumont, Jacques, *Montage Eisenstein*, trans. by Lee Hildreth, Constance Penley and Andrew Ross (London : BFI Publishing, and Bloomington: Indiana University Press, 1987).

Bordwell, David, *The Cinema of Eisenstein* (Cambridge, MA: Harvard University Press, 1993).

Goodwin, James, *Eisenstein, Cinema, and History* (Urbana: University of Illinois Press, 1993).

Ivanov, Viacheslav, 'Estetika Eizenshtejna' [Eisenstein's Aesthetics], in his *Izbrannye trudy po semiotike i istorii kultury* [Selected Writings on Semiotics and History of Culture] (Moscow: Shkola 'Iazyki russkoi kul'tury', 1998), vol. 1, pp. 141–378.

Lovgren, Hakan, *Eisenstein's Labyrinth: Aspects of a Cinematic Synthesis of the Arts* (Stockholm: Acta Universistis Stockholmiensis, 1996).

Leyda, Jay and Zina Voinov, *Eisenstein at Work* (New York: Pantheon House, 1982).

Meilakh, Mira, *Izobrazitelnaya stilistika pozdnikh filmov Eizensteina* [Visual Style in Eisenstein's Late Films] (Leningrad: Iskusstvo, 1971).

SOME ESSAYS ON DIFFERENT ASPECTS OF *IVAN* (CHRONOLOGICAL LISTING)

Kinder, Marsha, 'The Image of Patriarchal Power in *Young Mister Lincoln* and *Ivan the Terrible* Part I (1945)', *Film Quarterly*, vol. 39 no. 2, Winter 1986, pp. 29–49.

Christie, Ian, '*Ivan Groznii*', *Monthly Film Bulletin* vol. 54 no. 647, December 1987, pp. 382–3.

Kozlov, Leonid, 'The Artist and the Shadow of Ivan', in Richard Taylor and Derek Spring (eds), *Stalinism and Soviet Cinema* (London: Routledge, 1993), pp. 109–30.

Kleiman, Naum, '*Formula finala*' [The Formula of the Ending], in *Kinovedcheskije Zapiski* [Film Scholarship Annals], no. 38, 1998, pp. 100–32.

Nesbet, Anne, '*Ivan the Terrible* and "The Juncture of Beginning and End', in A. Lavalley and Barry P. Scherr (eds), *Eisenstein at 100: A Reconsideration* (New York: Rutgers University Press, 2001), pp. 292–304.

Neuberger, Joan, 'The Politics of Bewilderment', in Lavally and Scherr (eds), *Eisenstein at 100: A Reconsideration*, pp. 227–52.

Zholkovsky, Alexander, 'The Power of Grammar and the Grammar of Power', in Lavally and Scherr (eds), *Eisenstein at 100: A Reconsideration*, pp. 253–67.

ALSO PUBLISHED

If you would like further information about future BFI Film Classics or about other books on film, media and popular culture from BFI Publishing, please write to:

BFI Film Classics
BFI Publishing
21 Stephen Street
London W1P 2LN

BFI Film Classics '…could scarcely be improved upon … informative, intelligent, jargon-free companions.'
The Observer

Each book in the BFI Publishing Film Classics series honours a great film from the history of world cinema. With new titles published each year, the series is rapidly building into a collection representing some of the best writing on film. If you would like to receive further information about future Film Classics or about other books on film, media and popular culture from BFI Publishing, please fill in your name and address and return this card to the BFI.* (No stamp required if posted in the UK, Channel Islands, or Isle of Man.)

NAME

ADDRESS

POSTCODE

WHICH *BFI FILM CLASSIC* DID YOU BUY?

* In North America, please return your card to: Indiana University Press, Attn: LPB, 601 N. Morton Street, Bloomington, IN 47401-3797

C2

BFI Publishing
21 Stephen Street
FREEPOST 7
LONDON
W1E 4AN